SELF AND SOCIETY IN THE POETRY OF NICOLÁS GUILLÉN

SELF AND SOCIETY
IN THE POETRY
OF NICOLÁS GUILLÉN

LORNA V. WILLIAMS

THE JOHNS HOPKINS UNIVERSITY PRESS
BALTIMORE AND LONDON

This book has been brought to publication with
the generous assistance of the Andrew W. Mellon Foundation.

The Johns Hopkins University Press, Baltimore, Maryland 21218
The Johns Hopkins Press Ltd., London

Library of Congress Cataloging in Publication Data

Williams, Lorna V.
Self and society in the poetry of Nicolás Guillén.

(Johns Hopkins studies in Atlantic history and
culture)
Bibliography: pp. 163–74
Includes index.
1. Guillén, Nicolás, 1902-   —Criticism and
interpretation. I. Title. II. Series.
PQ7389.G84Z9   861   81-8404
ISBN O-8018-2666-7   AACR2

CONTENTS

PREFACE

The idea for this book was conceived during a sabbatical leave from Dartmouth College. While teaching modern Spanish-American literature, I was struck by the number of essays that referred to the importance of Guillén's work, yet book-length studies, the usual sign of an author's importance in the literary tradition, are virtually nonexistent on Guillén. Only four extensive studies have been published thus far. Several doctoral dissertations have been written, but until now, with the exception of a brief introductory work, no in-depth study has been available to English-speaking readers. Most of Guillén's work is available in translation, which makes Guillén seem familiarly unfamiliar to the English-speaking public; it also makes the need for a detailed study more apparent. This book, therefore, represents an attempt to fill the critical gap by taking a closer look at Guillén's major works.

Various aspects of Guillén's poetry have been studied from time to time. However, although several excellent essays have been written, they tend to focus, in general, either on Guillén's early work or on his most recent poetry. If the analyses of the early work tend to be purely stylistic, most serious studies of the latest poetry are essentially ideological. Given the fact that Guillén was as concerned with poetic technique as with presenting a wide range of human experience in his poetry, I have approached his work from an interdisciplinary point of view. In attempting to arrive at the meaning of specific verses within their cultural context, I have incorporated the findings of historians and social psychologists because mine is essentially an inquiry into the nature of perception.

The public nature of Guillén's poetic expression justifies the approach that I have taken to his work. Since Guillén has consciously assumed the role of spokesman for a pluralistic society, my study takes up the question of how one's position in society affects one's perception of that society, as well as how one's attitude to society affects the nature of one's communication about it. Given Guillén's ethnic background, I have found it necessary to examine his treatment of the African past and the situation of Afro-Cubans in order to see the degree to which cultural conditioning affects attitudes to the self. In addition to inquiring into the nature of the black self and its representation in poetic language, I have examined the general question of Cuban identity, particularly with regard to how the growth of a national consciousness was affected by Cuba's existence, first as a Spanish colony, and later as a dependency of the United States. The first part of the study is therefore an analysis of the impingement of the past on the present. In the second part of the study I examine Guillén's projections toward the socialist future as a means of overcoming the perceived alienation of the self from society. In view of Guillén's official position as president of the National Writers' Union, I also attempt to see how the coming of the Revolution has affected his choice of themes as well as his handling of them. The five major chapters on the changing concepts of the Cuban self and its representation are preceded by an Introduction where I examine the critical problems posed by Guillén's perceptions of the relationship between literature and society.

The manuscript became a reality thanks to the aid of several sources. The generous support of the Tinker Foundation and the Social Science Research Council enabled me to spend the 1978-79 academic year as a Fellow of the Program in Atlantic History and Culture at The Johns Hopkins University. Lively discussions with the members of the seminar sharpened my critical awareness of the dialectics of text and context, and I am grateful to my colleagues at Johns Hopkins for their invaluable comments on portions of the manuscript. Richard L. Jackson and Manuel Durán also offered helpful suggestions. A special debt of gratitude is owed to Franklin W. Knight, who not only guided the project from its inception, but also provided me with difficult to obtain Cuban materials and expert editorial advice.

I am also indebted to the staff of Dartmouth's Baker Library, especially Pat Carter, who cheerfully processed my interminable requests for materials through Interlibrary Loan. The staffs of the Hispanic Foundation at the Library of Congress and the Eisenhower Library at The Johns Hopkins University provided further bibliographical assistance. However, it is the expert typing skills of Barbara Harrington, Jane Meyer, and Theresa Orso of the University of Missouri–St. Louis, that ultimately enabled the manuscript to take shape.

SELF AND SOCIETY IN THE POETRY OF NICOLÁS GUILLÉN

CHAPTER 1

INTRODUCTION

Few writers are as representative of their times as the Afro-Cuban, Nicolás Guillén. Born in 1902, the year when his country became an independent republic, Guillén has lived through most of the significant moments in Cuba's recent history, except the years of the second Batista government, which he spent in exile.[1] Much of this collective experience is filtered through Guillén's poetic consciousness, and as a result, he was declared National Poet in 1961 by the current revolutionary regime.[2]

Guillén's work therefore poses a problem for critics whose concept of poetry is based on the self-referential nature of the poetic word. Many of Guillén's verses deal with blacks and the situation of the oppressed, whose very incorporation into a poetic text already shifts attention away from the purely linguistic dimension and points toward the context in which such categories as "the international proletariat" acquire social meaning. Occasionally the desire to speak of the world takes precedence over the careful selection of the means with which to represent it. But in general there is a judicious balance between expressive form and what is signified. In the case of a poet whose concern for the unemployed black is articulated for the most part in the traditional octosyllabic meter of Hispanic ballads, or who deploys a dazzling combination of rhyme, assonance, free verse, and poetic prose in an elegy to an assassinated labor leader, it is tempting to focus on the stylistic aspect of his work and to neglect its referential component.

To Cintio Vitier, for example, it is less significant that Guillén's early verses deal with blacks than that they successfully incorporate the musicality and spirit of the *son*.[3] That the particular rhythms on which Guillén patterned his work were the product of the Afro-Cuban sector was of little interest to Vitier, because, as he states, Cuban poetry is not only beyond ethnicity, but it is also "nontelluric."

Consequently, Guillén's representation of black speech patterns does not evoke the presence of blacks for Vitier, since a particular use of language is seen as the production of harmonious sounds by a disembodied consciousness, rather than as a means of situating oneself in the world. When language is dissociated from existence, a specific mode of expression is freed from its ethnic moorings and recuperated at a national level.[4]

A universalist version of Vitier's reading was given in a recent anthology, where it was stated that "Guillén has excelled in adapting the rhythms of Cuban popular speech and Afro-Cuban music in verse that nonetheless, for all its Caribbean charm, remains essentially in the traditional Spanish mold."[5] Here we have a variant of an earlier assessment of Guillén's poetry, which labeled the author of the *Cantos para soldados y sones para turistas* (Songs for Soldiers and Ballads for Tourists) as "a classic poet." Speaking of Guillén, Torres-Ríoseco pointed out that "with his extensive knowledge of Spanish literature, he has been able to give elegance and precision to Negro motifs."[6]

What Cintio Vitier, Torres-Ríoseco, and Rodríguez Monegal perceived to be an essentially Hispanic mode of expression was considered by another critic to be "a lyric poetry which is carrying on African traditions in a European language."[7] The very elements of Guillén's work—symbolic force, rhythmic stylistic devices—that were regarded by Vitier as signs of its fundamental Cubanness, and therefore of its transcendence of race,[8] now serve to place it firmly in the canon of traditional African poetry.[9]

Guillén's early verses were published at a decisive moment: the height of the avant-garde movement of the pre-World War II era. The causal links between the European cult of the primitive, the Harlem Renaissance, the scholarly investigations of Fernando Ortiz, and renewed interest in the black population of several New World countries have been carefully examined.[10] What was significant was that the poetic techniques used by Guillén—personification, daring metaphors, synesthesia, repetition, onomatopoeia, alliteration, and other verbal devices to simulate the sound effects of music, musical instruments, and dancing—served to identify him as the leading practitioner of *negrista* verse.[11] Once Guillén became identified as a creator of period pieces, this identification would affect critical reaction to his work.

Impressionistic studies have been made that designate Guillén as an ancestral voice whose spontaneous utterances are in marked contrast with the deliberate creations of other Latin American poets.[12] The poet himself has unwittingly contributed to the perpetuation of this stereotype by explaining in a much-quoted lecture that the composition of his first poems was not a conscious undertaking but rather the accidental materialization of sounds that imposed themselves on him while he was in a trance-like state.[13] Despite the fact that systematic studies would be made of the poet's linguistic virtuosity,[14] their formalistic emphasis still left the impression of Guillén as a mindless, "bongo-beating Orpheus."[15]

Interestingly enough, it is the early dialect poems that would be considered the essential Guillén by Gordon Brotherston, whose quest for a "pure" black poetry leads him to exclude from his purview all but Guillén's first two volumes of verse. Presumably, "the tradition of black poetry in Latin America" is here equated with the picturesque, since the poetic quality of Guillén's poems, which use standard Spanish to speak of the black situation, is dismissed as a valid criterion for regarding them as "the vehicle of a distinct consciousness."[16]

While Brotherston seems willing to consign the bulk of Guillén's poems to oblivion, more historically-minded critics would engage in a comprehensive look at his entire poetic output.[17] Although Ruscalleda's is the most ambitious study on Guillén to date, its poem-by-poem and book-by-book approach is little more than a tedious amassing of details, that uses no general principle other than chronology to organize the details into meaningful critical statements.[18] Since certain themes tend to recur in Guillén's poems, a sequential summary of their content cannot make a distinction between specific poems because it reduces all representations of a particular situation to the same referent.

Even as the formalists ignored or minimized the referential aspect of Guillén's work, other readers gave greater emphasis to the historicists' concern for conceptual meaning by presenting the ideas articulated in selected poems by Guillén as the major factor to be taken into consideration.[19] For Juan Marinello the fact that Guillén's poetry spoke not only of the world, but spoke to it with the intention of changing it, gave validity to his creative enterprise. And if to Torres-Ríoseco the words of Guillén's poetry had merely formal properties, and as such, were distanced from the world that they clearly represented, to Juan Marinello, the authenticity of Guillén's words derived from their being grounded in a specific ethnic reality and in a particular time and place. Poetic language was no longer set over and against its external points of reference, as postulated by the admirers of black Orpheus, since it was now believed that historical events could be shaped by the force of the poet's utterances.[20]

A detailed examination has already been made of the impingement of the abortive popular uprising against President Machado on Guillén's consciousness, and the effect that his becoming a Communist Party member in 1937 had on the course of his poetic development has been documented.[21] However, if certain critics did not seem to be troubled by Guillén's "Una canción a Stalin" (A Song to Stalin), which hailed Stalin as the champion of liberty, they would become troubled once Guillén began to write poems in celebration of Castro's Revolution. Undoubtedly the degree to which one shares the poet's perceptions of his role as that of voicing the experiences of his community will determine the extent to which one feels that artistic integrity is transgressed when poetic language is invested with documentary significance. Thus, while Lourdes Casal sees Revolutionary events as lying beyond the horizon of the speakable, José Antonio Portuondo believes that it is the transposition of political events into art that makes Guillén's poetic procedure that of a contemporary troubadour. The extra-linguistic reality called into being by certain poems that Casal judges to be "of very poor quality and very politicized,"[22] serves, in the opinion of Portuondo, to enhance their exemplary character as instances of revolutionary art.[23]

Recent translators seem to share Portuondo's assessment of Guillén's poetic enterprise. Thus, in one instance, the very poems that Lourdes Casal considers to be inherently flawed are the only compositions that are translated into English.[24] In the case of Robert Márquez, Guillén's major translator, Márquez's preference for works of a determinate content leads him to omit from his anthologies most of the *negrista* verses that Brotherston regards as Guillén's finest work.[25]

The transparency of their opening onto the world makes it difficult to separate the domain of social meaning from critical evaluation of Guillén's poems. At the same time, because expressive form remains a primary consideration for Guillén throughout his career, one should refrain from stressing the significance of his words, thereby neglecting the process through which meaning is articulated. Attending to the means of signification is particularly important in Guillén's case because so many of his poems seem to reject their condition as visual objects on the printed page.

Many of the poet's rhetorical strategies are intended to achieve the immediacy of speech in a medium that imposes a separation between writer and audience. At the outset, the desire to escape the silence of print is expressed overtly in the attempt to establish an orthographic equivalence between sight and sound. Yet, even when the orthographic conventions of script are respected, the thrust toward oral communication is still retained by the presence of a speaking subject and of dialogic situations that appear to reproduce the structures of spontaneous speech. The reader is thereby cast in the role of a participant in a verbal performance, despite his visual assimilation of Guillén's text.

Insofar as signs seek to evoke sounds in the mind of the reader, the poet attempts to erase the difference between the visual and the oral by restoring poetry to the status of a spoken utterance. Nevertheless, the problematic nature of this undertaking means that although both aesthetes and committed readers seem to respond to the sound of the poet's words, the aesthetes remain tied to visual principles of perception; thus their reading of Guillén is bounded by the spatial limits of the text. To content-oriented readers, on the other hand, Guillén's words name things in the existential world that are experienced as an immediate presence, resonating beyond the limits of the printed page.

Politically minded critics tend to perceive the continuity between word and world in terms of the adequacy of poetic representation in meeting the needs of the historical moment. Thus Guillén's timely elegy upon the death of Jesús Menéndez is hailed as the proper response of an artist to his social obligations. Inasmuch as the poem articulates the frustrations of the Cuban people in a language acceptable to both the political and the literary realms, it is said to have fulfilled the basic conditions of poetry as a force for national integration.[26] In this regard, several of Guillén's poems can be considered to be inscribed within the ethnopoetic project defined by Sylvia Wynter, for they constitute a conscious thrust toward the structuring of a communal self.[27]

As Roberto Fernández Retamar has noted, while Guillén's poems bear the mark of a personal style, very few of them are personal in the sense of being focused on the experiences of the individual self as an entity. For Guillén "assumes his collectivity as his own being," and by expressing the concerns of his society in verses that are, in turn, taken up by the Cuban people as anonymous creations, he succeeds in closing the gap between art and ordinary existence.[28] Thus, for folklorists, the question of the symbiotic relationship between word and world is not simply a matter of examining the degree to which poetry embodies political reality, or even of assessing the social function of poetry, but rather a matter of evaluating the aesthetic qualities of certain poems that lend themselves to becoming embedded in the popular consciousness. For example, in her comparative study on Guillén and Langston Hughes, Dellita Lowery concludes that despite the stylistic variations between poems like "Secuestro de la mujer de Antonio" (Seduction of Antonio's Wife), that derive from popular songs, and poems such as "Negro bembón" (Thick-lipped Black Man), that were subsequently set to music, both types of composition are sufficiently close in texture and structure to popular forms of artistic expression as to make them recognizable to their audience as an authentic elaboration of existing oral genres. Poetry is thereby considered to be a locus of cultural continuity, not only because it activates elements of past and present experience within its textual space, but also because its linkage with other modes of communication enables it to circulate among a wide audience.[29]

The conscious aim to bridge the spatial distance between reader and work makes much of Guillén's poetry occasional verse. Whether composed on the outbreak of the Spanish Civil War, or in commemoration of local events such as Fidel Castro's "Declaration-of-Havana" speech, certain poems possess an immediacy that could well have only historical interest when the event to which they refer has been forgotten by the majority of people. In fact, Keith Ellis has cited the tautological recapitulation of political language as one of the pitfalls of poetry that takes contemporary history as its referent, apart from the obvious problem of alienating readers who are unsympathetic to the encroachment of sociopolitical concerns upon poetic language.[30] On the other hand, Lowery sees the poetic recycling of contemporary issues as a necessary supplement to journalism in a society where knowledge and analysis of events in the world were not always available for popular comment.[31]

The need to engage his readers in the affairs of their time determines Guillén's choice of themes. If the poems of *West Indies Ltd.* speak of the problems of the present, other verses take up the question of how the colonial past and the legacy of slavery compound the difficulties of the present. And, as already noted by Juan Marinello, other poems envisage an alternative future. The cognitive intention that informs such poems often results in a discursive style. Indeed, an entire volume of poems, *El diario que a diario* (The Daily Newspaper), is cast in the form of a gazette in order to explore a series of events from the colonial past through the revolutionary present.

The concern for conceptual significance that marks such poems stems not only from a belief in the ability of poetry to effect a closure between word and being, as stated by Roberto Fernández Retamar, but also from a view of the poet as the privileged bearer of truth. In fact, in the *Sones para turistas* (Ballads for Tourists), the name of one of the poet's surrogates, José Ramón Cantaliso, is chosen because it corresponds to his function of singing about the plain truth. Ironically, critics like Brotherston, who prefer Guillén's early compositions, tend to perceive him as a creator of danceable poems. Yet the self-proclaimed mission of Cantaliso and some of the other dramatized selves of the poet is to compose ballads that are deliberately undanceable. While musicality will not always be absent from Guillén's poems, the ethical responsibility that he feels toward his readers means that he often strives to call attention to what had previously been passed over. Consequently, poverty, unemployment and other social inequities become fitting subjects for his poetry.

At the same time, the poet is not content with reflecting what he considers to be the true state of his society. He passes judgment on the events represented in his verses and becomes thereby the conscience of his people. In assuming this role, Guillén's premise is evidently that the poet is more discerning than the people whose cause he champions. While the populist tone that he often maintains is intended to erase all traces of condescension toward his implied audience, there is no doubt that his denunciation of selected patterns of behavior is, in effect, an attempt to alter the consciousness of his actual readers. Given the fact that the poet's perceptions were often contrary to the logical possibilities of the objective situation, particularly during the 1930s when there was little cause for optimism, one could easily call into question the underlying assumption of the poet as the voice of civic authority.

Subsequent events would give many of Guillén's words the retroactive status of prophecy. Yet, at the moment when the vision of social unity was first enunciated, it seemed to be only a rhetorical proposition, or at best the expression of a utopian ideal. However, once revolution became a historical possibility in Cuba, the poet's words from an earlier era could be seen as designating more than a metaphorical opening onto the future. For example, in a recent essay, Guillén's chief biographer, Ángel Augier, credits the poet with having foreseen as early as 1934 the arrival of a moment of social justice even though it still lay beyond the perceptions of the average Cuban.[32]

Alfred Melon would make even greater claims for Guillén's poetry by asserting that it played an instrumental role in the shaping of Cuba's revolutionary future. According to Melon, Guillén not only assessed correctly the ideological needs of his people at each stage of their long struggle for self-affirmation, but his verses also actively paved the way for a resolution of all the contradictions of social relations in Cuba as well as in Latin America and other societies where injustice exists.[33] Yet, as Keith Ellis reminds us, the claim that poetry has a direct impact on the evolution of a society is a dubious proposition because of the ambiguity inherent in the poetic act. Specifically, poems that seem to speak of, and to, the world ultimately remain enclosed within the verbal tradition of literature.[34] Rhyme, assonance, meter, imagery, and other stylistic elements combine to make even committed poetry more polyvalent than other forms of language intended to elicit action in the empirical world. Thus, as Melon himself recognizes, Guillén's mastery of poetic technique enables readers of widely divergent political views to appreciate his work, and in some instances, to ignore its extraliterary referent.[35]

While Melon may have overstated the case for the determining influence of Guillén's work on the course of Cuban history, he makes a valid point regarding the poet's engagement in the quest for an authentic Cuban identity.[36] Perceiving, as it were, a symbolic connection between the fortuitous coincidence of the year of his birth with that of the creation of the Cuban state, the poet sets himself the task of making his readers aware of their incompleteness. His assumption is that such an awareness would lead to his readers acquiring a sense that they constitute the Cuban nation. In Guillén's view, the achievement of political independence after decades of struggle did not mean that Cubans had acquired a genuine concept of self because they failed to perceive themselves as members of the new polity. As in the days of colonial rule, the social self continued to be mirrored through alien eyes.

Here Guillén's view seems to coincide with that of the "dependency theorists," who perceive Caribbean man as being defined primarily by the relations of political and economic dependency linking his country to Europe and/or the United States.[37] But such views perceive identity as a one-dimensional transaction, whereby Caribbean man is seen to exist only as a being for others without possessing a corresponding sense of himself. Apparently, incorporation into the international economic system has led to the decentering of the Cuban subject, who is now believed to exist solely through the recognition of the metropolitan other.

On the one hand, this presupposes a belief in the existence of an autonomous Cuban self prior to the arrival of the Europeans or the North Americans. And indeed, while pre-Columbian man lived untroubled by the thought of producing an agricultural surplus for a European market, the idea of an authentic self situated in an irrecoverable past not only reveals a nostalgia for lost unity, but also precludes the possibility that Cubans will ever exist for themselves. On the other hand, the presumed centrality of the metropolitan other to the constitution of the Cuban subject is predicated on an idealization of the Euro-American as pure subject. Presumably, once a country has been subordinated to the political and economic control of the metropolis, the residents of such a country are destined to introject the values of their colonial masters and thereby become permanently separated from the center of their own being. Discontinuity from the self in space is substituted for continuity with the self in time and space, in that desires generated in a distant metropolis come to be perceived as the organizing center of the national personality.

Yet, while Cuba's autonomy was circumscribed by its relations with Spain and subsequently with the United States, the view of the Cuban self as structured primarily by an alien presence presupposes the inability of Cubans to differentiate the self from the not-self. Not only would Cubans exist solely to be manipulated by others but, by virtue of the unbridgeable gap created between Cubans and their authentic selves by the arrival of the Europeans and the North Americans, they would remain frozen in the impossibility of experiencing themselves as complete persons. Their entire existence would be mediated by the Euro-American presence. And since all being would reside in the metropolis, Cubans would be condemned to remain fragments of European or North American men, who would appear to possess the solidity and coherence that the Cubans would be felt to lack. For Cubans, being would be a function of perception in that they would be unable to sustain a sense of their separateness from others and would feel compelled to have their existence validated by the presence of the Euro-American other. Inasmuch as Cubans would be only what they were perceived to be, absence from the other's regard would be equated with nonbeing. And since they would be constantly threatened with the dissolution of their being because of their inability to perceive themselves as individuals in their own right, Cubans would seek to overcome the threat of disintegration by appropriating aspects of the Euro-American self as their own.

However, to the very extent that Cubans would be felt to lack consistency because of their inability to sustain a sense of identity from their own resources, the desire for coherence would be an unrealizable ideal. For if identity is equated with otherness, and if self is confused with other, the dependence on the controlling consciousness of the Euro-American for self-realization would mean exile from the realm of self-determination. As a result of the colonial experience, autonomy would be forever out of reach, because the will to be would be replaced by the desire to be another. Actions could therefore not be taken as a sign of the Cuban subject's intentions toward his world because it would be assumed that the source of agency lay beyond the boundaries of the self.

The idea of the Cuban as a being separated from his own desires by the interposition of an alien authority would seem to imply that all that would be required for the attainment of true self-expression would be the dissolution of the metropolitan link. But if the metropolitan other is indeed as fundamental to the structuring of the Cuban self as the dependency theorists seem to indicate, the negation of that relationship would be in itself an act of self-mutilation. The fusion of self and other would mean that the other could not be suppressed without a corresponding threat of disintegration to the self. Moreover, if Cubans are considered to be fundamentally incapable of realizing intentional acts of their own because all action is seen as an embodiment of the desires of an alien authority, the possibility of Cubans becoming conscious historical actors is precluded from consideration. Assigning priority to metropolitan constraints in the determination of Cuban affairs implies a negation of the role of interiority in the shaping of the Cuban situation. For not only existing problems but also responsibility for their solution would be viewed as being causally located in the metropolitan center. And since it could be assumed that the metropolis would be opposed to Cubans' asserting their right to be, the prospect of autonomy becomes a dangerous illusion.

The static view of the opposition between center and periphery that undergirds the preceding argument denies historical validity to well over four hundred years of Cuban existence. It is a view espoused not only by Guillén in moments of despair, but also by dependency theorists who, despite their avowed intentions of understanding the situation of Third World people, predicate their understanding on a theory that privileges the metropolis in the constitution of the Latin American subject.[38] By referring the problems of the contemporary Latin American back to the moment of his insertion into the international capitalist order, this view endows a particular conjuncture of socioeconomic events with the status of an absolute origin, in reference to which all subsequent developments in Latin America must necessarily be regarded as a loss of plenitude. If the originating circumstances of the twentieth-century Cuban are assumed to be a primal lack, his status as a historical subject is clearly put into question, for all his intentional acts would already carry within themselves the mark of the original condition of nothingness. His actions would therefore have no real consequences, and thus all his post-Conquest activity would be emptied of significance.

Nevertheless, Guillén's perception of the Cuban self does not altogether deny him historical existence. If the insertion into the international economic order is felt to have resulted in a diminished mode of being, it is not considered to have totally precluded the possibility of meaningful action. A margin of freedom is perceived to be still available to the individual, despite his being determined by social structures that had come to dwell within him. Many of Guillén's poems are therefore intended to be appeals to the Cuban reader's margin of freedom in order to facilitate the pursuit of self-determined ends. And even though the nature of poetry makes it doubtful that Guillén's verses enabled the revolutionary changes of the Castro regime to become a historical possibility, the fact that many poems present a world that is altered over the centuries by the conscious acts of several persons indicates that the poet believes that the Cuban was not totally determined by socioeconomic structures beyond his control. By virtue of having acted to shape his environment, the Cuban asserted his historical presence in the world. Other poems point toward the prospect of revolutionary change, which confirms the view that Guillén ultimately believed that the Cuban self was not fated to be simply a distorted reflection of the metropolitan other.

Belief in the eventuality of revolutionary change presupposes that the Cuban is capable of assessing his situation objectively, and that he possesses the means for engaging in effective action so as to provide his social existence with a satisfactory content in accordance with his own desires. This would imply that the individual is aware that he is different from the other and that he perceives his actions to be an expression of his own intentions. Moreover, the possibility of becoming would be a goal that lay before the individual rather than being something that was forever closed to him.

Admittedly, socioeconomic circumstances impose constraints upon the individual's freedom to act. Once the individual is socialized, he becomes aware of his inability to alter significant areas of his daily existence. Nevertheless, the process of socialization involves not only an awareness that man is determined by structures beyond his control, but also a recognition by the individual of the possibilities for determining his own situation. Without an acknowledgement of the individual's capacity to act, the idea of human freedom becomes an illusion. Moreover, if the Cuban self is seen as being structured solely by external forces, it becomes impossible to explain the long struggle for sociopolitical independence, particularly in the light of the recent attempts by the revolutionary government to order the world according to Cuban priorities.

Even when one admits that the individual is free to act within certain clearly defined limits, it is apparent that the individual's capacity for meaningful action will vary according to his position within society, or according to his perception of that place. Recently emancipated slaves, for example, would be unlikely to have the same degree of control over their environment that the sons of their former masters possess. One would not expect, in a society stratified along ethnic lines, that the descendants of African laborers would readily perceive themselves to be the center of their world. Consequently, in the following pages, an attempt will be made to address the problem of self-perception and its relationship to the poetic presentation of the evolution of Cuban society. However, before arriving at a comprehensive view of the changing concepts of the Cuban self and its representation, it will be necessary to examine Guillén's treatment of the African heritage in order to see how the mulatto spokesman for a Eurocentric culture perceives the role played by Cuba in determining the adaptation of Africans to their conditions of existence in the New World.

Part One

THE
PRESENCE
OF THE
PAST

CHAPTER 2

THE
AFRICAN
PRESENCE

For most blacks living in the Americas, Africa is the continent from which one's ancestors came, but it is hardly the place where one seeks poetic inspiration in the present. Time and space remain frozen in that mythical primeval moment when one's ancestors were forced to embark on the slave ships traveling to the New World. Since few residents of the Americas have a first-hand knowledge of the land of their forefathers, popular fantasies of Africa form a standard part of the collective memory of black peoples in the New World. The presence that once was Africa has been displaced by Europe, as the languages spoken in the Americas so eloquently attest. And yet, centuries of miscegenation have failed to eliminate all traces of Africa from the sociocultural repertoire of blacks in the New World. Or rather, the awareness that one is no longer as one's ancestors were has often led blacks to assert their continuity with an ideal African past that predates contact with the "corrupting" influences of Euro-American civilization.

In this respect, Guillén's poetry is instructive. In the opening lines of the "Son número 6" (*Son* Number 6), the speaking subject declares himself to be Yoruba. However, by the middle of the second stanza, it becomes evident that the persona is no longer the representative of a particular ethnic group, but rather the spokesman for what M. G. Smith would term a generalized African culture:[1]

Yoruba soy,
cantando voy,
llorando estoy,

15

y cuando no soy yoruba,
soy congo, mandinga, carabalí.
[I am Yoruba,
singing along,
weeping,
and when I am not Yoruba,
I am Kongo, Mandinka, Calabar.]

("Son número 6," 1: 231)[2]

The poem thereafter becomes a celebration of that cultural convergence that has often been regarded as a characteristic of black societies in the New World. If, on the existential plane, ethnic identity becomes interchangeable, in rhetorical terms, the primacy of Yoruba culture is upheld through the force of repetition, thereby reflecting the cultural reality of Cuba.[3]

Frequent references to Shango, and mention of his wife, Oshun, whose protection is invoked even for Stalin, also serve to highlight the predominance of the Yoruba influence in Cuba. Since it is generally acknowledged that the religious domain has remained the most faithful reflection of the African presence in the New World, it is possible to regard the red beads worn by the black woman who dances through the pages of *Sóngoro cosongo* as a sign that she is a worshipper of Shango, and to note that one of his sacrificial foods, *quimbombó* (okra), the basic ingredient of a kind of stew, has become part of the national diet, which the nostalgic tourist dreams of in Paris.[4] As the "Balada del güije" (Ballad of the River-Spirit) makes clear, being a worshipper of Shango, or even wearing his insignia, does not offer unlimited protection against death or misfortune. It would appear that in this case the necklace has lost its mystical power and should have been specially treated by the priest so as to endow it with the miraculous power of the god that would have saved the child's life.[5]

It should be noted that the cause of death is not said to be the malfunctioning of the child's body, or even an accident. Instead, intentionality is attributed to the river, which is peopled with beings that devour black children and other passers-by. By granting the river a spiritual dimension, Guillén reveals his characters to be living in an anthropomorphic universe, as did the members of traditional African societies.[6] Since meaning is perceived in the objects of the natural world, which are often the dwelling-places of divinities, man is obliged to propitiate them to maintain harmony in the universe. In this case, words are used as incantation, for the mother hopes to dispel misfortune by repeating:

Ñeque, que se vaya el ñeque!
Güije, que se vaya el güije!

[Curse, may the curse go away!
River-spirit, may the river-spirit go away!]

("Balada del güije," 1:143–45)

Here the word, which ordinarily is believed to have the capacity to ward off disaster by virtue of its symbolic role as a means of transmitting divine power, has ceased to be effective, for it too seems to have lost its mystical force.[7]

That the word may possess this mystical power is amply demonstrated by "Sensemayá," the "chant for killing a snake." In this instance, the word is charged with sufficient spiritual force to produce the desired effect. Undoubtedly, the results of the chant depend on the manner in which it is uttered. In Guillén's hands, verbal expression attains the condition of music, as the author exploits the percussive possibilities in the name of one of the Kongo peoples to set the basic rhythm of the poem:

¡Mayombe—bombe—mayombé!
¡Mayombe—bombe—mayombé!
¡Mayombe—bombe—mayombé!

("Sensemayá," 1: 147–49)

While the octosyllabic meter of the choral repetitions serves as the frame of reference for the entire performance, the call-and-response structure of the poem makes polymeter possible, for verses of contrasting meters are used to mark the stages of the snake's progress. A syncopated rhythm is also achieved through the manipulation of a limited vocabulary, which depends for its effectiveness on the recurrence of set phrases with contrasting patterns of accentuation. This becomes most pronounced in the final stanza, where the heterophonic mode of the choral response marks the death of Sensemayá:

¡Mayombe—bombe—mayombé!
Sensemayá, la culebra . . .
¡Mayombe—bombe—mayombé!
Sensemayá, no se mueve . . .
¡Mayombe—bombe—mayombé!
Sensemayá, la culebra . . .
¡Mayombe—bombe—mayombé!
Sensemayá, se murió.

[Mayombe—bombe—mayombé!
Sensemayá, the serpent . . .
Mayombe—bombe—mayombé!
Sensemayá, is not moving . . .
Mayombe—bombe—mayombé!
Sensemayá, the serpent . . .
Mayombe—bombe—mayombé!
Sensemayá, it is dead.]

(1: 148-49)

The oral quality of the poem reveals its grounding in an African conception of the role of the human voice, which in musical composition is the primary instrument around which all others are centered.[8]

However, as Ruth Finnegan indicates, in verbal compositions that are sung, sound often takes precedence over sense, as the rhythmic requirements of the music make the use of nonsense words and onomatopoeia necessary.[9] Guillén's preference for the *jitanjáfora* in his early poetry is therefore in keeping with this widespread tendency of the African lyric. At the same time, it should be pointed out that whereas the lyric is only one of the many genres in African literature, and that while one of its characteristic features results from the subordination of meaning to melody, for many New World writers of Guillén's generation, the lyrical divorce between sound and sense comes to symbolize the nature of African man.

As G. R. Coulthard has observed, the Spenglerian atmosphere prevailing in Europe in the decade after the First World War was conducive to the adoption of such a stance, since many people who were disillusioned with European intellectual endeavor, as manifested by its death-dealing technology, were searching for an Adamic world in which being was no longer inhibited by thought.[10] Since Africa had always been perceived to lie on the periphery of Europe, which was the center from which all visions of culture were projected, it readily came to occupy that ideal space as a continent in which man lived in a state of nature, unencumbered by the processes of rational thought. To Caribbean writers who generally took their cue from Europe, and for whom Africa was equally out of focus, despite the fact that they were surrounded by living reminders of the African connection, the celebration of African spontaneity became a means of asserting their American vitality and originality in the face of the evident "decline" of Europe. According to O. R. Dathorne, ignorance and desire caused this literary vision of Africa to acquire the characteristics of a landscape of the mind,[11] since it was required to be everything that Europe was not.

Many of the prevailing attitudes toward Africa are present in

Guillén's early work. For example, the causes of the migration to the Americas are not sought in the internal structure of particular African societies, which would explain how many slaves arrived in the New World as a result of political expedience, socioeconomic necessity, or even human ruthlessness and greed, as recent scholarly research has since demonstrated.[12] Instead, as the "Balada de los dos abuelos" (Ballad of the Two Grandfathers) indicates, the African is portrayed as an innocent victim of superior European cunning, easily tempted by a few worthless beads into the holds of the slave ship. The pilgrimage to the Americas begins at an unlocalized point in space, where man has not yet imposed his imprint on the landscape. The hot, humid jungles teeming with monkeys and alligators therefore appear as a metonymic sign for a continent whose most distinctive feature is its primitiveness:

Africa de selvas húmedas
y de gordos gongos sordos . . .
— ¡Me muero!
(Dice mi abuelo negro.)
Aguaprieta de caimanes,
verdes mañanas de cocos . . .
— ¡Me canso!
(Dice mi abuelo blanco.)
Oh velas de amargo viento,
galeón ardiendo en oro . . .
— ¡Me muero!
(Dice mi abuelo negro.)
¡Oh costas de cuello virgen
engañadas de abalorios . . .!
— ¡Me canso!
(Dice mi abuelo blanco.)
¡Oh puro sol repujado,
preso en el aro del trópico;
oh luna redonda y limpia
sobre el sueño de los monos!

[Africa of the humid jungles
and big, muffled drums . . .
—I am dying!
(Says my black grandfather.)
Water blackish with alligators,
mornings green with coconuts . . .
—I am tired!
(Says my white grandfather.)
Oh ships sailing in a bitter wind,
galleon on fire for gold . . .
—I am dying!
(Says my black grandfather.)
Oh coasts of virgin necks

deceived with glass beads . . .!
—I am tired!
(Says my white grandfather.)
Oh pure, embossed sun,
imprisoned in the hoop of the tropics;
oh moon, round and limpid
above the sleep of monkeys!]

("Balada de los dos abuelos," 1: 138)

Here man and nature share the same unspoiled condition, as conveyed by the references to "virgin necks," "pure sun," and "limpid moon." Equally significant is the fact that the European grandfather is characterized by his eyes, the principal organ of perception, while the African grandfather is presented as an earthy, muscular creature:

Pie desnudo, torso pétreo
los de mi negro;
pupilas de vidrio antártico
las de mi blanco.

[Bare foot, stony torso
those of my black one;
pupils of antarctic glass
those of my white one.]

(1: 137)

Implicit in the vision of elemental strength embodied by the prototypical African ancestor is the idea of mindless energy, totally committed to a life of sensuality. In this connection, "Madrigal" comes readily to mind. To a certain extent, the poem can be regarded as merely a *machista* portrayal of the black woman:

Tu vientre sabe más que tu cabeza
y tanto como tus muslos.
Ésa
es la fuerte gracia negra
de tu cuerpo desnudo.

Signo de selva el tuyo,
con tus collares rojos,
tus brazaletes de oro curvo,
y ese caimán oscuro
nadando en el Zambeze de tus ojos.

[Your belly knows more than your head
and as much as your thighs.
That
is the strong black charm
of your naked body.

Yours is the mark of the jungle,
with your red necklaces,
your bracelets of curved gold,
and that dark alligator
swimming in the Zambezi of your eyes.]

                              ("Madrigal," 1: 121–22)

However, her metaphorical attributes reveal that her sensuality is
an atavistic quality, transmitted to her by her African forebears.

The aconceptual propensity of the African explains his willingness
to indulge in singing and dancing, preferably to the pulsating rhythms
of the drum. Add alcoholic stupor, and we have the major ingredients
of the then popular image of African man:

¡Yambambó, yambambé!
Repica el congo solongo,
repica el negro bien negro;
congo solongo del Songo
baila yambó sobre un pie.

Mamatomba,
serembe cuserembá.

El negro canta y se ajuma,
el negro se ajuma y canta,
el negro canta y se va.

Acuememe serembó,
                    aé;
               yambó,
                    aé.

Tamba, tamba, tamba, tamba,
tamba del negro que tumba;
tumba del negro, caramba,
caramba, que el negro tumba:
¡Yamba, yambó, yambambé!

[Yambambó, yambambé!
The Kongo solongo is ringing,
the black man, the real black man, is ringing;
the Kongo solongo from the Songo
is dancing the yambó on one foot.

Mamatomba,
serembe cuserembá.

The black man sings and gets drunk,
the black man gets drunk and sings,
the black man sings and goes away.

Acuememe serembó,

                         aé,
                      yambó,
                         aé.

Bam, bam, bam, bam,
bam of the black man who tumbles;
drum of the black man, wow,
wow, oh the black man is tumbling:
yamba, yambó, yambambé!]

                                    ("Canto negro," 1: 122-23)

"Canto negro" (Black Song) is no doubt one of the poems that Lloyd
King had in mind when he stated that Afro-Cubanism simply per-
petuates the stereotypical image of the black man as primitive.[13]
Indeed, the very form of the poem is the expression of its referential
dimension, for it defies translation because its semantic content is
minimal. It therefore establishes that the pleasure-seeking creature
that is its subject has a limited capacity to articulate meaningful sounds.

And yet, perhaps the isolated fragments of intelligible sound—
"congo," "Songo," "yambó"—correspond to what Edward Brathwaite
would perceive as a genuine desire to re-establish the link with Africa,[14]
particularly since, according to Fernando Ortiz, significant numbers
of the population who had been born in Africa were still living in
Cuba when Guillén came of age.[15] However, as George Lamming
has indicated, for the Caribbean writer who lives in a culture where the
dominant values are European-oriented, the attempt at reconnection
is problematic because Africa is so carefully screened from his conscious experience. The result is often a feeling of ambivalence.[16]
Guillén's poem, ironically entitled "Mujer nueva" (New Woman),
exemplifies this ambivalent attitude, for in his enumeration of the
positive qualities of this new African woman, he reduces her to an
animal-like status by referring to her "anca fuerte" (strong haunch)
(1: 120).

Undoubtedly, as Lamming has asserted, the dilemma of the Afro-
Caribbean writer stems from the fact that while he recognizes Africa's
contribution to the shaping of his own being, for him, Africa as historical and geographical entity has ceased to have a tangible existence.[17]
Consequently, as in Guillén's poem "La canción del bongó" (Song
of the bongo), the name, "Bondó," comes to represent absolute negativity:

        siempre falta algún abuelo,
        cuando no sobra algún Don
        y hay títulos de Castilla
        con parientes en Bondó:

[some grandfather *is always missing*,
when some Sir is not left over
and there are titles from Castile
with relatives in Bondó:]

("La canción del bongó," 1: 117)[18]

Since the negation of Africa also implies the negation of part of
his being, the Caribbean writer often attempts to fill the void with
"human significance."[19] But this attempt can be only partially successful, for in his engagement with that continent, the writer soon recognizes that he has lost the key to deciphering its true meaning. Names,
places, people, kinship systems, political affiliations, nationality—in
fact all the relationships that serve to anchor the self in a society—
have passed into a state of otherness. Hence the sense of loss so ad-
mirably expressed in Guillén's "El apellido" (The Family Name).
The crossing of the Atlantic has severed the links with those who
stayed behind; this explains the vaporous nature of the imagery each
time an effort is made to recall the point of origin:

¿Ya conocéis mi sangre navegable,
mi geografía llena de oscuros montes,
de hondos y amargos valles
que no están en los mapas?
¿Acaso visitasteis mis abismos,
mis galerías subterráneas
con grandes piedras hùmedas,
islas sobresaliendo en negras charcas
y donde un puro chorro
siento de antiguas aguas
caer desde mi alto corazón
con fresco y hondo estrépito
en un lugar lleno de ardientes árboles,
monos equilibristas,
loros legisladores y culebras?

[Do you already know my navigable blood,
my geography full of dark mountains,
of deep and bitter valleys
that are not on the maps?
Did you by chance visit my abysses,
my underground galleries
with big, damp stones,
islands jutting out from black pools
and where I feel a pure stream
of ancient waters
fall from my high heart
with a fresh and deep crash
into a place full of burning trees,

acrobatic monkeys,
legislating parrots and snakes?]

("El apellido," 1: 395)

No doubt because the new environment does not offer enough scope for self-actualization, there is a stubborn insistence on inscribing oneself in the original frame of reference:

¿Seré Yelofe?
¿Nicolás Yelofe, acaso?
¿O Nicolás Bakongo?
¿Tal vez Guillén Banguila?
¿O Kumbá?
¿Quizá Guillén Kumbá?
¿O Kongué?
¿Pudiera ser Guillén Kongué?

[Am I Yelofe?
Nicolás Yelofe perhaps?
Or Nicolás Bakongo?
Perchance Guillén Banguila?
Or Kumbá?
Maybe Guillén Kumbá?
Or Kongué?
Could I be Guillén Kongué?]

(1: 397)

However, the series of rhetorical questions points to the bewildering nature of such an undertaking. While the family names selected are indeed authentic, they represent groups widely separated on the continent, and so pose the problem of belonging, or rather no longer belonging, even more acutely.

The anguished search for roots has been created by a breakdown in the system of communication:

¿No tengo pues
un abuelo mandinga, congo, dahomeyano?
¿Cómo se llama? ¡Oh, sí, decídmelo!
¿Andrés? ¿Francisco? ¿Amable?
¿Cómo decís Andrés en congo?
¿Cómo habéis dicho siempre
Francisco en dahomeyano?
En mandinga ¿cómo se dice Amable?

[Don't I then have
a Mandinka, Congolese, Dahomean grandfather?
What is his name? Oh, yes, tell it to me!
Andrés? Francisco? Amable?

How do you say Andrés in Congolese?
How have you always said
Francisco in Dahomean?
In Mandinka, how do you say Amable?]

(1: 396)

Because he no longer speaks the language of his ancestors, the persona
is unable to share in those experiences that give families their cohesion,
and thereby signal his right to participate as a full-fledged member
of the family. Hence he can now refer only to "lejanos primos" (distant cousins) (1:398).

Yet despite their remoteness, he still claims a relationship with them.
However, the years of separation have resulted in an alteration of
perception. Acts performed in the new environment, which attempt
to retain what is assumed to be the spirit of the old, often take on
a new significance or undergo a shift in focus. This is noticeable in
the sphere of the dance. The rumba, for example, was originally a
neo-African secular festival dance that had several movements, and,
as with dance forms in Africa, was dramatic in orientation.[20] However, by the time Guillén wrote his poem "Rumba," even though
the dramatic focus of the dance was retained, the emphasis was placed
on the erotic element, to the exclusion of other sequences such as the
yambú, which mimed old age:

Pimienta de la cadera,
grupa flexible y dorada:
rumbera buena,
rumbera mala.

[Pepper of the hip,
flexible and golden rump:
good (female) rumba dancer,
bad (female) rumba dancer.]

("Rumba," 1: 123)

The above comments by the narrator are African in flavor in that
they reveal that the audience is not simply a passive spectator of the
performance by the dancing couple. Nevertheless, a new mode of
consciousness has intervened, which results in the simplification of
the rhythm of the music as well as in the reduction of the various
movements of the dance to the single movement of the *guaguancó*,
an attraction/repulsion dance of courtship.

A similar transformation can be observed in "Ébano real" (Royal
Ebony), which Olabiyi Yai has aptly defined as a praise poem.[21]
Indeed, the poem is structured on the principles of parallelism and

repetition, which, as Ruth Finnegan has observed, are marked features of praise poetry.[22] As is customary in poems of this genre, the first stanza extols the virtues of the tree:

> Te vi al pasar, una tarde,
> ébano, y te saludé:
> duro entre todos los troncos,
> duro entre todos los troncos,
> tu corazón recordé.
>
>> Arará, cuévano,
>> arará sabalú.
>
> [On passing by one afternoon, I saw you,
> ebony, and I greeted you:
> hard among all trunks,
> hard among all trunks,
> I remembered your heart.
>
>> Arará cuévano,
>> arará sabalú.]

("Ébano real," 1: 229)

But in the rest of the poem, a disproportionate number of stanzas are devoted to the pursuit of a reward by the panegyrist:

> --Ébano real, yo quiero un barco,
> ébano real, de tu negra madera . . .
> Ahora no puede ser,
> espérate, amigo, espérate,
> espérate a que me muera.
>
> [--Royal ebony, I want a boat,
> royal ebony, from your black wood . . .
> It can't be now,
> wait, my friend, wait,
> wait until I die.]

(1: 229)

While there are instances in African literature when the panegyric will include the direct request for a reward from the patron, particularly in the more democratic societies where the poet has to survive by his own initiative and enterprise rather than through royal patronage,[23] the emphasis there is still on validating and affirming the status of the patron, and not, as in Guillén's poem, on boldly highlighting the profit motive.

In emphasizing the profit motive, perhaps Guillén wishes to convey an idea of the exploitative nature of relationships in the Caribbean.

Needless to say, the Americas are not the only area where exploitation occurs, since Africa too has proved vulnerable in that regard. Not only were parts of the continent ravaged in the past to supply workers for the mines and plantations of the New World, but even in the twentieth century Europe has continued to impose its will on the African continent.

That this is invariably a violent situation is clearly seen from the title of Guillén's poem, "Soldados en Abisinia" (Soldiers in Abyssinia). In Mussolini's case, the desire to restore the empire of the Caesars leads to the incorporation of Ethiopia in the Italian sphere of influence. But in Guillén's opinion, this gesture will ultimately be unsuccessful because it is founded upon an abstraction:

> El dedo, hijo de César,
> penetra el continente:
> no hablan las aguas de papel,
> ni los desiertos de papel,
> ni las ciudades de papel.
> El mapa, frío, de papel,
> y el dedo, hijo de César,
> con la uña sangrienta, ya clavada
> sobre una Abisinia de papel.

> [His finger, child of Caesar,
> pierces the continent:
> the paper waters do not speak,
> nor do the paper deserts,
> nor do the paper cities.
> The cold, paper map,
> and his finger, child of Caesar,
> with its bloody nail, already stuck
> on a paper Abyssinia.]

>   ("Soldados en Abisinia," 1: 185)

In his self-aggrandizement, Mussolini evidently did not consider the possibility of local resistance to this threat to Ethiopian national sovereignty. There is, therefore, a contrast between the passivity of the "paper Abyssinia" envisaged by Mussolini and the dynamism displayed by a country determined to resist colonial penetration:

> Abisinia se encrespa,
> se enarca,
> grita,
> rabia,
> protesta.

[Abyssinia gets angry,
becomes confused,
shouts,
rages,
protests.]

(1: 186)

By attributing the actions to the country as a whole rather than to individuals, Guillén implies that this is a mass movement for liberation.

Nevertheless, the defensive actions taken by the Ethiopians are clearly ineffectual, even if they are energetic. But instead of underscoring the Ethiopian defeat, Guillén emphasizes the high cost of victory to Italy in human lives:

Entonces, los soldados
(que no hicieron su viaje sobre un mapa)
los soldados,
lejos de Mussolini,
solos;
los soldados
se abrasarán en el desierto,
y mucho más pequeños, desde luego,
los soldados
irán secándose después lentamente al sol,
los soldados
devueltos
en el excremento de los buitres.

[Then, the soldiers
(who did not travel on a map)
the soldiers,
far from Mussolini,
alone;
the soldiers
will be burnt up in the desert,
and much smaller, of course,
the soldiers
afterwards will go on withering slowly in the sun,
the soldiers
returned
in the excrement of the vultures.]

(1: 187)

Moreover, for Guillén, the Italian-Ethiopian War is not simply a confrontation between colonizer and colonized; it also represents a class conflict within the ranks of the colonizers:

Mussolini, bañado,
fresco,
limpio,
vertiginoso.
Mussolini, contento.
Y serio.

¡Ah, pero los soldados
irán cayendo y tropezando!
Los soldados
no harán su viaje sobre un mapa,
sino sobre el suelo de África,
bajo el sol de África.
Allá no encontrarán ciudades de papel;
las ciudades serán algo más que puntos que hablen
con verdes vocecitas topográficas:
hormigueros de balas,
toses de ametralladoras,
cañaverales de lanzas.

[Mussolini, bathed,
fresh,
clean,
dizzy.
Mussolini, happy.
And serious.

Ah, but the soldiers
will go on falling and stumbling!
The soldiers
will not travel on a map,
but on the soil of Africa,
under the sun of Africa.
There they will not find paper cities;
the cities will be something more than dots that speak
with little green topographical voices:
swarms of bullets,
coughs of machine-guns,
canefields of lances.]

(1: 186-87)

By contrasting the cool calculations of Mussolini, who is isolated from
the main theater of events, with the harsh realities encountered by his
soldiers, Guillén suggests that the Italian soldiers who go to their deaths
in Ethiopia are the unwitting executors of a policy that is contrary to
their own interests. The implication is that like the Ethiopians, these
soldiers are victims of a misguided imperialist decision.

If "Soldados en Abisinia" hints at the similarity of conditions among the ranks of the oppressed, and therefore offers the prospect of their potential solidarity irrespective of race, culture, or national origin, "Mau-Maus" is exclusively concerned with advocating self-determination for the African victims of colonial oppression. Guillén reveals the Mau Mau to be engaged in an unequal combat against the British settlers, who, supported by their government, use their military and technological superiority, as well as their control of the print media, to overwhelm the Kikuyu fighters physically and psychologically. Dual interpretations of the same event reflect the existence of a compartmentalized colonial world, "inhabited by two different species," already described by Fanon:[24]

Envenenada tinta
habla de los mau-maus;
negros de diente y uña,
de antropofagia y totem.
Gruñe la tinta, cuenta,
dice que los mau-maus
mataron a un inglés . . .
(Aquí en secreto: era
el mismo inglés de kepis
profanador, de rifle
civilizado y remington,
que en el pulmón de África
con golpe seco y firme
clavó su daga-imperio,
de hierro abecedario,
de sífilis, de pólvora,
de money, business, yes.)

[Poisoned ink
speaks of the Mau Mau;
blacks of tooth and nail,
of anthropophagy and totem.
The ink grunts, relates,
says that the Mau Mau
killed an Englishman . . .
(Confidentially speaking: it was
the same Englishman with the violating
shako, with civilized
rifle and Remington,
who in the lung of Africa
with a dry, firm stroke
stuck his dagger-empire,
of alphabet iron,
of syphilis, gunpowder,
of money, business, yes.)]

("Mau-Maus," 2: 32)

The fundamental conflict of interests leads to seemingly absurd gestures
on the part of the Mau Mau:

> Tinta de largas letras
> cuenta que los mau-maus
> arrasan como un río
> salvaje las cosechas,
> envenenan las aguas,
> queman las tierras próvidas,
> matan toros y ciervos.
> (Aquí en secreto: eran
> dueños de diez mil chozas,
> del árbol, de la lluvia,
> del sol, de la montaña,
> dueños de la semilla,
> del surco, de la nube,
> del viento, de la paz . . .)
>
> Algo sencillo y simple
> ¡oh inglés de duro kepis!
> simple y sencillo: dueños.
>
> [Long-typed ink
> tells that the Mau Mau
> wreck the harvests
> like a savage river,
> poison the waters,
> burn the productive lands,
> kill bulls and deer.
> (Confidentially speaking: they were
> owners of ten thousand huts,
> of the tree, of the rain,
> of the sun, of the mountain,
> owners of the seed,
> of the furrow, of the cloud,
> of the wind, of peace . . .)
>
> Something plain and simple
> Oh Englishman with the hard shako!
> simple and plain: owners.]

(2: 33-34)

But the apparently illogical "strategy of immediacy"[25] that the Mau Mau
adopt is in fact a dramatization of their need for a more just sociopolitical order. Through their disruption of the agricultural economy,
they manifest their refusal to participate in a system that ascribes to
them a permanently inferior status. In their attempt to negate the
conditions of existence defined for them by the British other, the Mau

Mau have taken the first step toward what René Depestre would define
as a process of "dezombification,"[26] as they strive to recover the land
and liberty taken from them by the British.

It is significant that Guillén refers to the group by the name "Mau
Mau," which, according to Kenneth Grundy, was never used by its
members to designate themselves, but rather was a term "more generally
employed by Europeans, their governments, and their press."[27] By a
technique of ironic reversal, already studied by Antonio Olliz Boyd in
another context,[28] Guillén gives this originally derogatory term a more
positive valuation, for he reveals the British to be capable of far greater
savagery than the Kikuyu whom they denounce:

> Letras de larga tinta
> cuentan que los mau-maus
> casas de sueño y trópico
> británicas tomaron
> y a fuego, sangre, muerte,
> bajo el asalto bárbaro
> cien ingleses cayeron . . .
> (Aquí en secreto: eran
> los mismos cien ingleses
> a quienes Londres dijo:
> —Matad, comed mau-maus;
> barred, incendiad Kenya;
> que ni un solo kikuyus (sic)
> viva, y que sus mujeres
> por siempre de ceniza
> servida vean su mesa
> y seco vean su vientre.)

> [Abundant-inked type
> relate that the Mau Mau
> took British tropical
> dream houses
> and by fire, blood, death,
> under the barbarous assault
> one hundred Englishmen fell . . .
> (Confidentially speaking: they were
> the same one hundred Englishmen
> to whom London said:
> —Kill, eat Mau Mau;
> sweep away, burn Kenya;
> let not a single Kikuyu
> live, and let their women
> see their tables
> forever served with ashes
> and their wombs barren.)]

(2: 32-33)

What the British perceive as a "constitutional depravity"[29] in the nature of the Mau Mau is thereby revealed to be a political response to a situation that denies the Kikuyu the right to be.

If Guillén's ethnic background, as well as the sociocultural composition of contemporary Cuba, serve to maintain his interest in the problems of twentieth-century Africa, there is no doubt that for him the historical process is irreversible. Although he acknowledges the continuity of the past in the present, he projects a vision of Africa that is not entirely situated in the mythical dimension but is also subject to the forces of contingency. Hence the multiplicity of African images evident in his work. The manifestation of the African presence displayed by the "Balada del güije" (Ballad of the River-Spirit) coexists with a lament for its absence in "El apellido" (The Family Name), while the stereotypical portrait of the primitive African appears side by side with its polar opposite in "Mau-Maus," and the timeless, landless perception of the "Balada de los dos abuelos" (Ballad of the Two Grandfathers) exists alongside of the particularistic, historical vision of "Soldados en Abisinia" (Soldiers in Abyssinia). Racial heritage, as well as common human experiences and ideals, make it possible for the poet to capture the African continent in a variety of attitudes. But, because Guillén is cognizant of the effects of time and history, his interpretation is grounded in a recognition of his own difference. Hence there is no attempt at a facile identification. The essential perspective on Africa remains that of "a Yoruba from Cuba."

CHAPTER 3

THE SITUATION OF BLACKS IN PREREVOLUTIONARY CUBA

Guillén's admission that he is "a Yoruba from Cuba" acknowledges that there are traces of the African presence in the cultural landscape of twentieth-century Cuba; it also indicates the discontinuity that the voyage to the New World introduced into the African mode of being. Even as the Yoruba succeeded in asserting their dominance among the various immigrant groups, they were, in turn, subordinated to the will of the Europeans. Since rulers and ruled in the New World were distinguished by race, religion, language, and culture, as well as by socioeconomic factors, it was virtually impossible for the African immigrants and their descendants to modify their subordinate status. Even though blacks had been in Cuba since the early sixteenth century, Africans continued to be an alien element in Cuban society until 1866,[1] and, like most black workers in Cuba, they lacked the absolute individual status of persons until 1886.[2] Thus it was possible for persons of African descent to appear to be human fragments until well into the twentieth century.

Persons engaged in the arduous tasks of the sugar plantation were simply perceived as "hands." And, as the opening lines of Guillén's "Elegía a Jesús Menéndez" (Elegy to Jesús Menéndez) indicate, by 1948 the human figure of blacks had become so abstract that the emotions that one would expect to find in the sugar workers are transferred instead to the sugar cane that they harvest:

Las cañas iban y venían
desesperadas, agitando
las manos.
Te avisaban la muerte,

[The canes came and went
desperate, with trembling
hands.
They warned you of death,]

("Elegía a Jesús Menéndez," 1:416)

The language of the poem conveys well the degree to which workers in the cane fields are reduced to their instrumental function:

alguna vez anduve con Jesús transitando de
sueño en sueño su gran provincia llena de hombres
que le tendían la mocha encallecida;

[once I went with Jesús travelling from
dream to dream over his great province filled with men
who stretched out their calloused machetes to him;]

(1: 425)

The customary gesture of greeting is attributed here to the work tool rather than to the hands wielding it, while the physical deterioration resulting from the nature of the work performed is registered by machetes, which appear to have become extensions of the bodies of the cane cutters.

The familiar association of black hands and machetes means that when these hands cease to perform their traditional function, the social standing of their owner is invariably that of the superfluous man. Thus, the open hands of Guillén's Sabás are an indication of his position on the fringes of his society:

Yo vi a Sabás, el negro sin veneno,
pedir su pan de puerta en puerta.
¿Por qué, Sabás, la mano abierta?
(Este Sabás es un negro bueno.)

[I saw Sabás, the black man without anger,
beg for his bread from door to door.
Why the open hand, Sabás?
(This Sabás is a good black man.)]

("Sabás," 1: 140)

Sabás's ineffectualness is highlighted by the rhetorical question, which recurs in the first three stanzas of the poem, thereby bringing into focus the attributes assigned to the beggar by collective opinion in the parenthetical statements. The explicitly pejorative content of the second set of adjectives applied to Sabás—"loco" (crazy), "bruto" (stupid)—gives a retroactive valorization to the quality initially ascribed to him by the term, "bueno" (good), and therefore causes his lack of indignation to appear as a sign of his complicity in his own degradation. Sabás's passive acceptance of his marginal economic role stems from his inability to project his sights beyond the immediate satisfaction of his biological needs. Hence the attempt of the speaking subject to defer the surrender to the demands of the body:

> ¡Caramba, Sabás, que no se diga!
> ¡Sujétate los pantalones,
> y mira a ver si te las compones
> para educarte la barriga!

> [Gee, Sabás, let it not be said!
> Get a hold of your pants,
> and try to see if you can manage
> to train your belly!]

(1: 141)

Presumably, the movement away from mere bodily satisfaction would generate a questioning attitude and lead to an examination of the underlying reasons for his actual social status. A desire for social advancement, which would first be manifested in more assertive gestures, would be expected to ensue. Once the persona began to express himself positively, he would not only erase the servile image that he had previously projected, but he would also acquire a heightened sense of self-respect.

Nevertheless, the material situation of blacks like Sabás explains the logical priority of their preoccupation with the body. As Frantz Fanon has observed, the closure of their socioeconomic possibilities has shifted the locus of identity for blacks and resulted in the "epidermalization" of their situation.[3] In other words, the limits imposed on their social participation has produced a visual image of the social self. In the following hypothetical dialogue, for example, Guillén's would-be lovers are highly conscious of their physical appearance:

> Ya yo me enteré, mulata,
> mulata, ya sé que dise
> que yo tengo la narise
> como nudo de cobbata.

Y fíjate bien que tú
no ere tan adelantá
poqque tu boca e bien grande,
y tu pasa, colorá.

Tanto tren con tu cueppo,
tanto tren;
tanto tren con tu boca,
tanto tren;
tanto tren con tu sojo,
tanto tren.

[I just found out, mulatto woman,
mulatto woman, I now know that you say
that my nose is
like a bow tie.

And look, you
ain't so light,
'cause your mouth is well big,
and your nappy hair, dyed.

All those airs with your body,
all those airs;
all those airs with your mouth,
all those airs;
all those airs with your eyes,
all those airs.]

("Mulata," 1: 104)

Yet, what should be simple statements of fact are enunciated rather forcefully in the text. In the presumed enumeration of genetic attributes, each has transformed aspects of the other's appearance into terms of abuse, placing thereby a misleading emphasis on the skin as the repository of specific values. At the very center of the term "adelantá" (light)[4] there is embedded the idea of progress, which implies an acceptance by the male persona of what H. Hoetink has defined as "the white somatic norm image,"[5] and which automatically consigns all those possessing visibly negroid features to be considered as a regressive social force.

Evidently, the characters have assumed the class distinctions prevailing in Cuban society of the time. But while the larger society must rely on the distribution of political power, wealth, and education to establish its hierarchy of prestige, Guillén's characters have few tangible means of marking social differences among themselves. Since they are inserted in a social order where the evidence of differential status is masked by a more obvious polarization along the axis of race, the human body easily becomes a primary indicator of social rank. A greater or lesser degree of blackness therefore comes to have more than personal significance. She who is mulatto, though otherwise undistinguished, automatically assigns herself a higher social status than is accorded the black man by virtue of her closer approximation to the phenotype of the dominant others. And in dyeing her hair, she seeks to give symbolic expression to that biological approximation, and thus distance herself from the darker members of her race. The black speaker, on the other hand, claims to have recognized her alienation from her biological reality and to have rejected her for this self-estrangement:

> Si tú supiera, mulata,
> la veddá;
> ¡que yo con mi negra tengo,
> y no te quiero pa na!

> [Mulatto woman, if you only knew
> the truth;
> that I am satisfied with my black woman,
> and I don't want you at all!]

(1: 104)

Yet, even if one concedes, as does Dellita Lowery, that in the light of the final stanza, the poem ultimately constitutes "an affirmation of racial pride,"[6] the fact is that the features that presumably render the love object attractive are the very ones used earlier by the speaker as the basis for deflating the mulatto woman's pretensions. Since the speaker is himself visibly negroid, this suggests that his own relationship with his body is a problematic one.

However, it is the addressee of the following lines who reveals the problem in all its complexity:

> ¿Po qué te pone tan brabo,
> cuando te disen negro bembón,
> si tiene la boca santa,
> negro bembón?

> [Why do you get so mad
> when they call you thick-lipped black man,
> if your mouth is beautiful,
> thick-lipped black man?]

("Negro bembón," 1: 103)

Here the self is clearly dissociated from the body, whose basic features are not experienced as a primary part of the person, but instead are perceived as embarrassing accessories that compare unfavorably with an ideal body image. The character's relationship with the very center of his being is therefore disrupted by the mediation of an alien mode

of self-evaluation, which causes the body as it is to appear imperfect
and therefore shameful. The term, "bembón" (thick-lipped),[7] even
though descriptively accurate, is interpreted as a sign of otherness,
no doubt because it seeks to refer the persona back to an African
origin that would render him an exotic presence in the Cuba of the
1920s. Thus, consciousness seeks to efface an ethnic identity that the
body discloses. Nevertheless, the futility of the desire to shift the
ground of racial identification is revealed at the level of poetic structure,
where the position of the heavily-accented phrase, "negro bembón"
(thick-lipped black man), calls attention to the very quality that the
character wishes to negate. Not only is the phrase "negro bembón"
made emphatic by its positioning in the first stanza of the poem, but
in the call-and-response structure of the third verse, where it functions
as a refrain, its unvaried repetition attains a percussive quality, which
serves as a persistent reminder of the persona's unalterable physical
condition even as the alternating statements about his psychological
and material condition vary in melodic content, though not in rhythm.

At the same time, it is possible that the character's frustration with
his genetic endowment stems from his inability to use his body as a
means of establishing his presence in the world. Lacking a job, one of
the principal modes of affirming his social existence, the addressee
thus comes to view with resentment the features that are considered
to serve as a pretext for excluding blacks from the labor market. A
precarious hold on social reality would therefore explain the need
for the functional domestic arrangement existing between the *bembón*
and Caridad:

> Bembón así como ere
> tiene de to;
> Caridá te mantiene,
> te lo da to.
>
> Te queja todabía,
> negro bembón;
> sin pega y con harina,
> negro bembón;
> majagua de dri blanco,
> negro bembón;
> sapato de do tono,
> negro bembón . . .
>
> [Thick-lipped just as you are,
> you got everything;
> Caridá keep you,
> she give you everything.
>
> Still you complain,

thick-lipped black man;
no gig and with bread,
thick-lipped black man;
white drill suit,
thick-lipped black man;
two-tone shoes,
thick-lipped black man . . .]

(1: 103)

But if the persona's woman spares him the need for concern about his material necessities, she is incapable of sparing him his sense of dissatisfaction at the incongruity of his actual mode of being with his desired status. The flashy clothes that she buys him merely serve to distract attention momentarily from that part of the body that he feels to be flawed, even as the grudging admiration that they evoke points to his partial success in imposing his subjectivity on the world.

It is readily apparent that the *bembón's* desire to be someone other than himself derives less from his anxiety about his anomalous masculine role than from his sense of biological inadequacy, for his notion of selfhood is not centered primarily on the performance of social acts. In cases such as the following, it is the more traditional expectation that he effectively assume the position of breadwinner that constitutes a threat to the subjectivity of the male persona:

Búcate plata,
búcate plata,
poqque no doy un paso má:
etoy a arró con galleta,
na má.
Yo bien sé como etá to,
pero biejo, hay que comé:
búcate plata,
búcate plata,
poqque me boy a corré.

Depué dirán que soy mala,
y no me quedrán tratá,
pero amó con hambre, biejo,
¡qué ba!
Con tanto sapato nuebo,
¡qué ba!
Con tanto reló, compadre,
¡qué ba!
Con tanto lujo, mi negro,
¡qué ba!

[Get money,
get money,

for I am not taking another step:
I am down to rice and biscuit,
that's all.
I quite realize how things are,
but, old man, you got to eat:
get money,
get money,
'cause I am going to split.

Then they will say I am evil,
and they won't want to deal with me,
but love and starvation, old man,
what bull!
With all those new shoes,
what bull!
With all those watch, brother,
what bull!
With all those fine things, brown sugar,
what bull!]

("Búcate plata," 1: 107-8)

Lacking money, which was the social symbol of masculinity in the
Cuba of the 1920s,[8] the rhetorically present male character becomes
an emotional liability because he is incapable of providing his woman
with the basic consumer goods that are placed temptingly on display
so as to make them seem accessible to everyone. The conspicuous
exaltation of materialism in the society makes a mockery of the idea
of romantic love binding a couple whose daily round of existence
takes place in the gap between the perception of unlimited possibilities
for accumulation and the reality of limited puchasing power. Terms
of endearment—"biejo" (old man), "compadre" (brother), "mi negro"
(brown sugar)—proliferate, even as they are emptied of emotional
significance by the realities of the economic situation. Although the
woman who uses them is conscious of the reasons for her impoverish-
ment, her will to survive precludes the adoption of the helpless stance
that her partner's silence appears to indicate.

The frequent repetition of the command, "búcate plata" (get
money), heightens the sense of urgency in the woman's exposition. As her
most persistent thought, it retains its salience by its unique syllabic
structure in the poem. Moreover, when each of her calls for material
gratification receives the same choral response—"¡qué ba!" (what
bull!)—it is the previously enunciated concept of food-starved love
that is actually being displaced to a secondary level, while her intensi-
fying demands for worldly goods are simultaneously given primary
stress. The tension between affection and enlightened self-interest
is thereby resolved in the latter's favor, although the poetic expression

of that resolution appears inconclusive, since the list of calls for consumer goods could easily be extended indefinitely.

The male persona's silent complicity in his own humiliation is replicated in other instances where the will to self-improvement is equally absent. Or rather, the constraints of their existential situation frequently undermine the desire of such persons to engage in meaningful activity. Because the immediacy of their problems looms so large in their perceptions, the prospect of their being able to solve those problems tends to recede from view. As a result, theirs is a static sense of time, with their existence unfolding in an eternal present. Or, in the case of the residents of the tenement house, they themselves come to be perceived as inert objects:

> — . . . Y éste es Luis, el caramelero;
> y éste es Carlos, el isleño;
> y aquel negro
> se llama Pedro Martínez,
> y aquel otro,
> Norberto Soto,
> y aquella negra de más allá,
> Petra Sardá.
> Todos viven en un cuarto,
> seguramente
> porque resulta barato.
> . . . .
>
> —Y la que tose, señores,
> sobre esa cama,
> se llama Juana:
> tuberculosis en tercer grado,
> por un resfriado
> muy mal cuidado.
> La muy idiota pasaba el día
> sin un bocado.
>
> ["And this is Luis, the candy man;
> and this is Carlos, from the islands;
> and that black man,
> his name is Pedro Martínez,
> and that other one,
> Norberto Soto,
> and that black woman over there,
> Petra Sardá.
> They all live in one room,
> certainly
> because it is cheap.
> . . . .
>
> "And the one, gentlemen, coughing

on the bed,
her name is Juana:
third-stage tuberculosis,
because of a very poorly treated
cold.
The silly fool went all day
without a bite."]

("Visita a un solar," 1: 203)

Despite the fact that each is mentioned by name, the name fails to make them personally unique, since it is the category of social illness that they represent that serves to make them distinctive. The relationships of consanguinity, which usually bind the individual residents of the *solar*,[9] are here replaced by a syntactical link between men and women, the sick and the healthy, the unemployed Afro-Cuban and the destitute immigrant. Consequently, the *solar* comes to seem less like a place of residence than like an institution for housing the casualties of an inequitable social system.

Admittedly, there are black slum residents who experience their situation as sheer negativity. Overwhelmed by the objective conditions of their existence—chronic unemployment or underemployment, substandard housing, poor health care, inadequate diet—they acquire so immutable a notion of social processes that they fail to perceive that these are subject to human manipulation. And even though they participate in the economic life of the society, they show little lucid awareness of belonging to the polity.

Perhaps the political disengagement of Afro-Cubans in the 1920s was due to their memory of a racial identity vigorously denied political expression in 1912 by a young republic determined to project itself as a homogeneous nation.[10] In a multiracial situation, blacks as such are relegated to the status of nonbeing, and so the idea of their organizing for self-improvement along racial lines is barred from consideration. Without a forum for articulating their particular concerns within the legal framework of the nation, blacks like the following speaker become convinced of their inability to act:

Mira si tú me conose,
que ya no tengo que hablá:
cuando pongo un ojo así,
e que no hay na;
pero si lo pongo así,
tampoco hay na.

[See if you understands me,
for it is no longer necessary for me to speak:
when I do one eye like this,

it means there is nothing;
but if I do it like this,
there still ain't nothing.]

("Hay que tené boluntá," 1: 106-7)

A consciousness incapable of embodying itself in language is deprived of the opportunity of inventing projects for itself, for the lapse into gestures implies the loss of a system for constituting social meanings. Where speech is regarded as superfluous, the possibility of summoning objects into existence ceases to exist because the conceptual categories that transform movements into actions are ultimately supplied by words.

Lacking the means of evoking things in their materiality, Guillén's persona adopts a fatalistic attitude toward the events of his life:

¡Hay que tené boluntá,
que la salasión no e
pa toa la bida!

[One must be strong,
'cause bad luck won't last
forever!]

(1: 107)

The persona perceives the will not as the faculty of intention, but as the capacity for enduring seemingly immutable social conditions. The supernatural interpretation of his situation places the locus of responsibility for its modification beyond his control, and by definition, prevents a realistic assessment of the structural forces that have contributed to his position. As a result, the impulse to engage in effective action for improving his material condition is held in abeyance.

But while Guillén's persona appears reconciled to his lack of mastery in the public domain, he maintains a narcissistic orientation to reality in the domestic sphere. Not only does he recommend that his woman place his personal interests above their mutual concerns, but he assigns her the primary task of seeing to their economic well-being:

Empeña la plancha elétrica,
pa podé sacá mi flú;
buca un reá,
buca un reá,
cómprate un paquete' vela
poqque a la noche no hay lu.

[Pawn the electric iron,
in order to take out my suit;
get a dime,

get a dime,
buy a pack of candle
'cause there ain't no electricity come tonight.]

(1: 107)

In establishing his list of priorities, he allows his suit to take precedence over items of domestic value, no doubt because the suit is expected to serve as a protective cover for an ego of diminished social stature. But in his self-preoccupation, he fails to realize that his domestic situation is intimately related to his appearance in the world. His inattention to domestic services means that he no longer has the mechanisms—iron and electricity—for maintaining his public image.

In shifting the burden of economic responsibility onto the woman's shoulders, the speaker evidently assumes that she is a figure of inordinate resourcefulness. Yet, there is also a recognition of the limitations on her ability to find a satisfactory solution to their problems. Instead of envisaging her as a being who attains concrete objectives, the poem ends with her portrayal as a body in constant motion:

Camina, negra, y no yore,
be p'ayá;
camina, y no yore, negra,
ben p'acá;
camina, negra, camina,
¡que hay que tené boluntá!

[Walk on, black woman, and don't cry,
go over there;
walk on, and don't cry, black woman,
come over here;
walk on, black woman, walk on,
for one must be strong!]

(1: 107)

Thus, purpose disappears once the primacy of movement dispels the notion of intention from human conduct.

The speaker's ability to propel the woman from place to place on the basis of his utterances suggests that his inadequacy as a provider bears no relationship to the degree of influence that he wields in his household. While the woman's tears imply a recognition of the futility of her movements, her evident compliance with the man's orders represents an endorsement of his right to dominate in the domestic realm. In such instances, where the social affirmation of the male self is inhibited by the malfunctioning of the national economy,[11] it is apparently considered more appropriate to express one's subjectivity by asserting control over the actions of one's female partner than it is to attempt to make the existing sociopolitical structure more responsive to one's needs by seeking a place within it. The larger problem of economic well-being is thus subordinated to the play of sexual differences, as the domestic arena becomes the primary space in which the question of male self-esteem is taken up.

It is characters like the *chévere* (dandy) who assume this orientation in its most radical form. Long separated from his sacred origins as a *ñáñigo*,[12] Guillén's *chévere* carries the *ñáñigo's* traditional devaluation of women[13] to an extreme because of his need to make the symbols of his masculinity highly visible:

> Chévere del navajazo,
> se vuelve él mismo navaja:
> pica tajadas de luna,
> mas la luna se le acaba;
> pica tajadas de canto,
> mas el canto se le acaba;
> pica tajadas de sombra,
> mas la sombra se le acaba,
> y entonces pica que pica
> carne de su negra mala.

> [Dandy of the knife thrust,
> becomes himself a knife:
> he cuts up slices of the moon,
> but the moon is fading out on him;
> he cuts up slices of song,
> but the song is fading out on him;
> he cuts up slices of shadow,
> but the shadow is fading out on him,
> and then he cuts up, oh he cuts up
> the flesh of his evil black woman.]   ("Chévere," 1: 125)

The structure of the poem reflects the centrality of performance to the *chévere's* whole way of life, in its expressive progression from his initial stylized gestures to the culminating act of violence in the final line. However, for the woman involved, the waning moon is already a sign of the imminence of death,[14] as is the assonant rhyme scheme—"navaja," "se le acaba," "negra mala"—in which the concepts of knife, dying, and woman come to be linked.

It is significant that the label "mala" (evil) provides the only indication of the reasons for her death. And yet, the veiled accusation of infidelity contained in that adjective is not made explicit, since the hypothetical rival is conspicuously absent from the text. It would appear that in this instance sexual aggressiveness from another is less to be feared than conveying an impression of weakness by failing to act as a self-respecting *macho*,[15] for the idea of the woman's sexual freedom evidently constitutes a threat to the *chévere's* manhood. Indeed, the use of the possessive, "su" (his), indicates that she has no autonomy, but rather, as depersonalized "flesh," she is merely an object possessed by him. As his property, she exists only to be acted upon by him. And since the *chévere's* existence is geared toward asserting his presence in the world, for him loss of face is an eventuality to be avoided at all costs. Consequently, once his woman is thought to have exceeded the bounds appropriate to the maintenance of his self-image, the *chévere* sees himself obliged to act to recover his prestige. Lacking the intellectual, economic and legal resources by which other men seek to resolve conflicts with their women, he resorts to his knife as the ultimate weapon of arbitration.

And yet, as Fanon has observed, such sporadic acts of violence generally mask more deep-seated anxieties. For men like the *chévere*, who belong to the underclass of their society, the social distance between themselves and the dominant others makes it imperative, in their view, to receive instant confirmation of their existence as men. Hence they adopt flamboyant postures in order to attract attention to themselves. However, the limited range of their capacity for self-disclosure creates feelings of frustration, which necessarily find release in aggressive acts.[16]

While such desperate attempts at reading the signs of their masculinity in the eyes of others tend to be cathartic, these acts usually fail to satisfy the demand for respect ultimately desired by their performers. In this respect, the *chévere* is reminiscent of the vengeful slave who also sought to affirm his manhood by an act of aggression:

Látigo,
sudor y látigo.

El sol despertó temprano
y encontró al negro descalzo,
desnudo el cuerpo llagado
sobre el campo.
. . . .

Después, el cielo callado,
y bajo el cielo, el esclavo
tinto en la sangre del amo.

Látigo,
sudor y látigo,

> tinto en la sangre del amo;
> látigo,
> sudor y látigo,
> tinto en la sangre del amo,
> tinto en la sangre del amo.
>
> [Whip,
> sweat and whip.
>
> The sun rose early
> and found the barefooted black man,
> his naked, wounded body
> on the ground.
> . . . .
>
> Later, the silent sky,
> and beneath the sky, the slave
> stained in the master's blood.
>
> Whip,
> sweat and whip,
> stained in the master's blood;
> whip,
> sweat and whip,
> stained in the master's blood,
> stained in the master's blood.]
>
> ("Sudor y látigo," 1: 227–28)

Here manhood is not a question of sexual identity but a more fundamental demand for recognition as a person. Yet, the ending of Guillén's
poem hardly leads one to concur with the assessment that the slave's
violent repudiation of the assaults on his body constitutes an "assertion
of manhood and human dignity."[17] The obsessive recurrence of the
symbols of oppression (sweat and whip), and of the final image of the
slave soiled by his master's blood, indicates that the slave's psychic
balance has been impaired by overexposure to degradation. Hence he is
incapable of making the transition to a state of freedom. If the master's
death is seen as the necessary antecedent to personal independence,
the act of killing him offers no prospect for self-enhancement, because
even in death the master continues to occupy a privileged place in the
mind and body of the slave. The violent act has become an end in itself,
and the slave still has no effective mode of advancing his claim for
proper consideration beyond the preliminary stage of negating an
undesired status.

Guillén's slave undoubtedly derives from his creator's "catastro-
phist" view of the Afro-Cuban past,[18] which perceives the slave's entire
existence as a pendular shift between the twin poles of overwork and

punishment. As a result, the slave is presented as having been so brutalized by his experience that even when he takes active steps to resist further dehumanization, he remains in a state of existential terror at the prospect of his own freedom. At the same time, Guillén's presentation contains an element of historical realism, in that the intention of a single slave to bring an end to his unfreedom was not likely to yield positive results in a slave-based economy. As Franklin Knight has indicated, the resources of pre-Abolition Cuba were as committed to restraining the hostile impulses of slaves toward their masters as to the production of sugar for profit.[19] Thus, for the slave the problem of self-realization was not only a question of activating a long repressed desire to be free from the indignities of life on the sugar plantation, but also a matter of coping with the real danger of unleashing the punitive forces of a slave society in the wake of an attack on the inviolable person of the master.

Even the most well organized conspiracies were unlikely to succeed where the individual thrust toward autonomy had failed. Slaves, by definition, lacked the fighting power of their owners, and so the real or imagined attempts of an Aponte or a Plácido to lead them in a struggle to recover their freedom by destroying the masters' lives and property could only end in disaster. The unpreparedness of the slave to engage in a conscious program of resistance is depicted by Guillén in "Noche de negros junto a la Catedral" (Black People's Night near the Cathedral) as a metaphorical state of exposure:

> Tambor.
> Resuena la noche ancestral.
> Vestidos de limpio, la risa desnuda,
> cien negros (o más, ¿cuántos son?)
> bailan a la luz de la Luna
> en la vieja plaza de la Catedral.
> Siglo XVIII, tal vez. Pero,
>   ¿y el cañaveral?

> [Drum.
> The ancestral night resounds.
> In clean clothes, open laughter,
> a hundred blacks (or more. How many are they?)
> dance by the light of the Moon
> in old Cathedral square.
> Eighteenth century, perhaps. But
>   what about the canefield?]
>   ("Noche de negros junto a la Catedral," 2: 286)

Nevertheless, throughout the centuries, slaves would strive to make an insurrectional leap to freedom against overwhelming odds. It is their repeated failures in this regard that led Guillén to condense well over two hundred years of existence in Cuba into a long, unbroken night.

When the moment came for a redefinition of the status of blacks in Cuba, it had less to do with their continuous efforts to disrupt the functioning of the plantation economy than with other political and technological developments that rendered obsolete the practice of using human energy as the primary motor force for the productive workings of the sugar mill.[20] As a result, the ex-slaves were hardly in a position to ensure that the terms of their emancipation worked to their advantage. Because they were absent from the deliberations that would establish the basis for their admission to full citizenship in their American homeland, it is not surprising that, some fifty years later, one of their descendants would be able to lament as follows:

> Yo,
> negro Simón Caraballo,
> y hoy no tengo qué comer.
> La mujer murió de parto,
> la casa se m'enredó:
> yo,
> negro Simón Caraballo,
> ni toco, ni bebo, ni bailo,
> ni casi sé ya quien soy.
> Yo,
> negro Simón Caraballo,
> ahora duermo en un portal;
> mi almohada está en un ladrillo,
> mi cama en el suelo está.
> . . . .
>
> No sé qué hacer con mis brazos,
> pero encontraré qué hacer:
> yo,
> negro Simón Caraballo,
> tengo los puños cerrados,
> tengo los puños cerrados,
> ¡y necesito comer!
>
> [I,
> black Simón Caraballo,
> and I have nothing to eat today.
> My wife died in childbirth,
> I was tied up in litigation over my house:
> I,
> black Simón Caraballo,
> neither play, nor drink, nor dance,
> I almost don't know who I am now.
> I,

black Simón Caraballo,
now sleep in a vestibule;
I have a brick for a pillow,
my bed is on the ground.

. . . .

I don't know what to do with my arms,
but I will find something to do:
I,
black Simón Caraballo,
have my fists clenched,
have my fists clenched,
and I need to eat!]

("Balada de Simón Caraballo," 1: 154)

The persona's repeated references to the self represent an attempt to shore up a faltering sense of identity. Because his hands appear superfluous, he is unable to create a place for himself in the present. All his activities belong to a previous moment.

Presumably, men like Simón Caraballo should no longer have cause to feel alienated from their society because constitutional changes have now granted them the same rights and duties enjoyed by all other members of the community. However, with the loosening of the persona's ties to the larger society, which is signaled by the loss of food, wife, and home, the idea of his equality before the law can only be experienced as a negative right: he is no longer able to sleep in vestibules:[21]

— ¡Simón, que allá viene el guardia
con su palo y su revólver,
y con el odio en la cara,
porque ya te oyó cantar
y te va a dar por la espalda,
cantador de sones viejos,
marido de tu guitarra. . . !
(Simón se queda callado.)

Llega un guardia de bigotes,
serio y grande, grande y serio,
jinete en un penco al trote.
— ¡Simón Caraballo, preso!

(Pero Simón no responde,
porque Simón está muerto.)

["Simón, here comes the policeman
with his stick and his revolver,
and with hatred in his face,
because he already heard you sing,
and he is going to hit you over the shoulder,

you, singer of old ballads,
wedded to your guitar. . . !"
(Simón remains silent.)

A policeman with a mustache arrives,
big and serious, serious and big,
mounted on a trotting nag.
"Simón Caraballo, under arrest!"

(But Simón does not answer,
because Simón is dead.)]

(1: 155)

Law enforcement agents are thus perceived as hostile to the Afro-Cuban's very existence.

Even soldiers, the designated defenders of the nation from its external enemies, are seen as the implacable enemies of the Afro-Cuban:

Soldado no quiero ser,
que así no habrán de mandarme
a herir al niño y al negro,
y al infeliz que no tiene
qué comer.

[I don't want to be a soldier,
so they will not have to send me
to hurt the child and the black man,
and the poor man who has nothing
to eat.]

("Soldado así no he de ser," 1: 183)

And although the army under Batista provided one of the few avenues of mobility available to blacks,[22] the soldier here is viewed as the natural oppressor of the Afro-Cuban, no doubt because he is a member of an institution whose primary duty until 1959 was the protection of foreign lives and property at the expense of the interests of the domestic population,[23] among whom black workers were by far the most vulnerable element.[24]

The syntactic adjacency of the black man and the child in the verse cited above recalls the minority status often attributed to blacks. But if the Afro-Cuban's economic situation is usually one of dependence, the sociopolitical dimensions of that dependence are a factor that blacks are forced to take into consideration very early in life. Thus, even the young are burdened by a collective history that robs them of their childlike quality:

Negrazo, venga
con su negraza.
. . . .

Negrón, negrito,
ciruela y pasa,
salga y despierte,
que el sol abrasa,
diga despierto
lo que le pasa. . .
¡Que muera el amo,
muera en la brasa!
Ya nadie duerme,
ni está en su casa:
¡coco, cacao,
cacho, cachaza,
upa, mi negro,
que el sol abrasa!

[Big and ugly nigger, come
with your big and ugly negress.
. . . .

Black man, black child,
plum and kinky hair,
come out and wake up,
for the sun is scorching hot,
say smartly
what is happening to you. . .
May the master die,
may he burn to death!
Now no one is sleeping,
no one is at home:
goblin, gobbling,
portion, potion,
up, up, my black one,
for the sun is scorching hot!]
                        ("Canción de cuna para despertar a un negrito," 2: 14-15)

Turning on its head the Ballagas poem that serves as its epigraph, Guillén's cradlesong is not intended to lull the hypothetical black child to sleep, but rather to arouse him to the harshness of his present reality. The inverted order of the usual movements of waking up and sallying forth underscores the importance of social awareness in the Guillén poem. The reassuring voice of the mother, who was solicitous of her child's welfare is gone, and there is no one in whose eyes the child is beautiful. Instead there is the shrillness of a bird, calling attention to the social disabilities of being black. The proliferation of racial terms: "negrazo" (big and ugly nigger), "negrón" (black man), "negrito" (black child), "negro" (black one), which range from the pejorative to the purely descriptive, succeeds in transforming the color of the child's skin into a kind of tragic flaw. As a result, the idea of the glorious future that informed the Ballagas poem is here rendered unthinkable. Even though slavery has long been abolished, the name of the master still retains its terrifying symbolic power because that aspect of the collective past is perceived as a present and not as a prior state. In G. R. Coulthard's words, slavery has become a metaphor for continued social injustice.[25] Consequently, Guillén's child is being socialized to conform to a preestablished place in society. And the closure of his existential possibilities is signified by the unrelenting rays of the sun.

Small wonder that characters like Papá Montero are made to escape the bleakness of this constricted world through a life of eternal parties. With the release offered him by music, dancing, sex, and rum, Papá Montero is presumed to exist at a remove from the claims of a humiliating past:

> Quemaste la madrugada
> con fuego de tu guitarra:
> zumo de caña en la jícara
> de tu carne prieta y viva,
> bajo luna muerta y blanca.
>
> El son te salió redondo
> y mulato, como un níspero.
>
> Bebedor de trago largo,
> garguero de hoja de lata,
> en mar de ron barco suelto,
> jinete de la cumbancha:
>
> [You left the wee hours smoking
> with the fire of your guitar:
> cane juice in the cup
> of your black and living flesh,
> beneath the deathly white moon.
>
> The ballad flowed out of you round
> and brown, like a naseberry.
>
> Swigging drinker,
> tin-plated gullet,
> boat adrift in a sea of rum,
> master of the orgy:]

("Velorio de Papá Montero," 1: 125–26)

The character's flight from awareness is reflected in the quality of his music which, though it excites admiration for its formal perfection, is likened to "a naseberry," and is thereby marked as a product for sensual consumption. Given the centrality of the pleasure principle to Papá Montero's whole way of life, the poem focuses on his body only in order to designate its various parts as instruments of pleasure. At the same time, the very intensity of the hedonistic thrust contains an element of tragic excess, whose mark is already revealed in the tense of finality in which the character is addressed and in the sign of the "dead moon" under whose light he undertakes his activities. The presence of the moon serves to link Papá Montero's world with that of the *chévere,* as does the atmosphere of violence in which he loses his life:

> En el solar te esperaban,
> pero te trajeron muerto;
> fue bronca de jaladera,
> pero te trajeron muerto;
> dicen que él era tu ecobio,
> pero te trajeron muerto;
> el hierro no apareció,
> pero te trajeron muerto.
>
> Ya se acabó Baldomero:
> ¡zumba, canalla y rumbero!
>
> Sólo dos velas están
> quemando un poco de sombra;
> para tu pequeña muerte
> con esas dos velas sobra.
>
> [They were waiting for you in the tenement,
> but they brought you in dead;
> it was a drunken brawl,
> but they brought you in dead;
> they say he was your brother,
> but they brought you in dead;
> the knife was not to be found,
> but they brought you in dead.
>
> Now Baldomero is all finished:
> clear out, scoundrel and rumba dancer!
>
> Only two candles are
> burning away a little of the shadow;
> for your insignificant death
> those two candles are more than enough.]

(1: 126-27)

For Papá Montero is also a *ñáñigo,* albeit a rather materialistic one. The movement away from the binding principles of the secret society is indicated by the fact that Papá Montero's murderer is the fellow initiate who should have been his chief defender.[26] Moreover, his wake, which should have been an occasion for elaborate funeral rites so as to ensure him a peaceful life in the hereafter,[27] has diminished in importance.

As a *ñáñigo* Papá Montero receives scant attention from his peers; as a ballad composer he is given a more fitting tribute by the poet, who eulogizes him in the *son*-like structure of the verse cited above.[28] Furthermore, the formal aspect of his music serves to give his life a more transcendental dimension:

> Y aun te alumbran, más que velas,
> la camisa colorada
> que iluminó tus canciones,
> la prieta sal de tus sones
> . . . .
>
> Hoy amaneció la luna
> en el patio de mi casa;
> de filo cayó en la tierra
> y allí se quedó clavada.
> Los muchachos la cogieron
> para lavarle la cara,
> y yo la traje esta noche
> y te la puse de almohada.
>
> [And they still illuminate you, more than candles,
> the red shirt
> which lit up your songs,
> the black charm of your ballads
> . . . .
>
> Today the moon arose
> in the patio of my house;
> it fell to the earth on its side
> and there it remained stuck.
> The boys took it
> to wash its face,
> and I brought it tonight
> and made it your pillow.]

(1 : 127)

The implication here is that through the quality of his art the character eventually rises above the dissipation of his material existence. His passing becomes an event of cosmic importance when the moon falls to earth and is made to serve as his pillow, thereby reversing the earlier insignificance of his death.

The ambivalence that marks Guillén's treatment of Papá Montero is also evident in his portrayal of the boxer in "Pequeña oda a un negro boxeador cubano" (Small Ode to a Black Cuban Boxer). The mock admiration for Papá Montero's drinking ability is here extended to the muscles that have made the boxer successful:

Ese mismo Broadway,
que en actitud de vena se desangra
para chillar junto a los rings
en que tú saltas como un moderno mono elástico,
sin el resorte de las sogas,
ni los almohadones del clinch;
. . . .

De seguro que tú
no vivirás al tanto de ciertas cosas nuestras,
ni de ciertas cosas de allá,
porque el training es duro y el músculo traidor,
y hay que estar hecho un toro.
como dices alegremente, para que el golpe duela más.
. . . .

En realidad acaso no necesitas otra cosa,
porque como seguramente pensarás,
ya tienes tu lugar.
Es bueno, al fin y al cabo,
hallar un punching bag,
eliminar la grasa bajo el sol,
saltar,
sudar,
nadar,
y de la suiza al shadow boxing,
de la ducha al comedor,
salir pulido, fino, fuerte,
como un bastón recién labrado
con agresividades de black jack.

[That very Broadway
which, like a vein, bleeds profusely
to scream beside the rings
in which you leap like a modern rubber monkey,
without resorting to the ropes,
nor the cushions of the clinch;
. . . .

Of course you
do not happen to be aware of some of our business,
nor of some business over there,
because the training is rough and the muscle treacherous

and one must be as strong as a bull,
as you say happily, in order to make the punch hurt more.

. . . .

In fact, maybe that's all you need,
because as you no doubt will think,
you already have your place.
It's fine, after all,
to find a punching bag,
lose weight in the sun,
leap,
sweat,
swim,
and from the fight to shadow boxing,
from the shower to the dining room,
come out polished, fine, strong,
like a freshly carved cane
with the aggressiveness of a blackjack.]

("Pequeña oda a un negro boxeador cubano," 1: 118–120)

The cult of the body, so appropriate in the case of an athlete, merely serves to indicate the degree of the boxer's mindlessness. To a certain extent, Guillén's representation of the boxer, like his portrait of Papá Montero, owes its focus to the current of primitivistic neo-Romanticism pervading the 1920s, which made one-dimensional treatment of blacks virtually obligatory.[29] Yet here too, as in the case of Papá Montero, Guillén inserts an element of tragedy that denudes the boxer's body of the sensuality so exalted by the Negrophiles of the 1920s. The animalistic comparisons point not in the direction of self-indulgence, but at an other-directed existence which, even in its finest hour, is perceived only as an entertainment machine for others.

While the objectivistic language is in keeping with Guillén's view of the boxer as an animalized robot, the intellectual deficiencies that it attributes to the boxer are not considered to be innate, but rather are the result of an inadequate education. This educational lack is said to be reflected in the boxer's speech:

Tu inglés,
un poco más precario que tu endeble español,
sólo te ha de servir para entender sobre la lona
cuanto en su verde slang
mascan las mandíbulas de los que tú derrumbas
jab a jab.

[Your English,
a little more shaky than your weak Spanish,
only has to be good enough for you to understand on the canvas
whatever the jaws of those you knock out

jab by jab
mutter in their
gross slang.]

(1: 119)

Interestingly enough, in referring to the quality of the boxer's speech, the poem does not attempt to speak from the place that the boxer effectively occupies in Cuban society, as in the case of the *bembón* (thick-lipped black man) and the *mulata*. No longer is there an effort to establish a phonetic equivalence between language and culture by means of such features as the assimilation and epenthesis of consonants (*cobbata, quedrán*) which, whether viewed as an attempt to render "transfers from African type phonological systems,"[30] or simply as a literary convention with little correspondence to actual Afro-Cuban speech,[31] are, in any event, an index of social marginality.

The convergence toward the grammatical patterns of standard Spanish has little to do with the fact that the boxer's fists have placed him in the mainstream of his society, which the *bembón's* joblessness did not do. A content of subordination is still being expressed in the grammar of dominance. At the same time, the strategy of reducing the salience of ethnic identity, even to the point of dispensing with lexical items such as "ecobio" (brother), is not regarded as a dissolution of the ties of racial solidarity because concern for expressive authenticity continues to be voiced:

Y ahora que Europa se desnuda
para tostar su carne al sol
y busca en Harlem y en La Habana
jazz y son,
lucirse negro mientras aplaude el bulevar,
y frente a la envidia de los blancos
hablar en negro de verdad.

[And now that Europe is stripping itself
to tan its flesh in the sun
and seeks in Harlem and Havana
jazz and *son*,
to be black and proud while the boulevard cheers,
and before the envy of whites
talk real black talk.]

(1: 120)

It could well be that Guillén's switching from a language that is ethnically distinctive to one that is ethnically unmarked is a response to the pressures of cultural assimilation exerted by a society that perceives as scandalous efforts to convey racial consciousness in a code that diverges from that of the norm.[32] The defensive tone of Guillén's prologue to *Sóngoro cosongo,*[33] which signals the elimination of the more overt markers of linguistic particularity from his poetry, would therefore appear to be an attempt to silence those critics who had greeted the dialectal aspect of his first poems with hostility.[34]

On the other hand, it appears that the movement toward the language of the dominant culture corresponds to a shift in the poet's perception of the situation of Afro-Cubans. In the atmosphere of political and economic crisis pervading the late 1920s, the sense of being estranged from the national institutions was no longer seen by Guillén to be an experience peculiar to black slum residents. The latter were simply a "colony within the colony,"[35] and, as we shall see in the following chapter, the dominance of Cuba's economy by the United States generated a feeling of alienation among various segments of the population and occasioned some of Guillén's most strident verse. The parallelism established between the exploitation of the boxer's fists and of Cuba's canefields therefore represents one of the poet's first attempts to link the fortunes of blacks with the fate of the nation:

> ese mismo Broadway
> que unta de asombro su boca de melón
> ante tus puños explosivos
> y tus actuales zapatos de charol;
> ese mismo Broadway,
> es el que estira su hocico con una enorme lengua húmeda,
> para lamer glotonamente
> toda la sangre de nuestro cañaveral.

> [that very Broadway
> which smears its melon-mouth with amazement
> at your explosive fists
> and your stylish patent leather shoes;
> that very Broadway,
> is the same one that stretches out its snout with an enorme wet tongue,
> to lick gluttonously
> all the blood in our canefield.]

(1: 118–19)

As Guillén ceased to focus on the black condition in isolation, the language of his poetry shifted from the use of signifiers of marked social differentiation to the use of signifiers of social inclusiveness. His choosing to refer to the boxer's divergent speech style in standard Spanish should be viewed as a preliminary step in the process of articulating a national consciousness.

CHAPTER 4

THE
COLONIAL
EXPERIENCE

Regardless of the nature of their
activities, the blacks of Guillén's pre-Revolutionary poetry all share
a condition of secondariness that points to an existence that depends
on the will of others for its validity. Despite four hundred years of
residence in the Americas, Afro-Cubans are perceived as "citizens
of the future,"[1] since there seems to have been little improvement
in their situation. From Guillén's point of view, the only difference
that events like the abolition of slavery and Cuba's declaration of
political independence have wrought on the lives of blacks is that
praise of the elemental strength of the muscular slave has given way
to praise of the muscular vigor of the dockworker or to celebration
of the mindless energy of the professional athlete, and that the overcrowded *solar* has been substituted for the cramped quarters of the
slave ship. Indeed, even though sentiments like the racial shame of the
bembón and the *mulata*'s color consciousness are attitudes specifically
generated in the New World environment, where political segmentation
along racial lines was manifested in its most complex form, for some of
Guillén's black characters the experience of living in the Americas
was regarded not as an original juncture, but rather as a provisional
state, akin to exile.

The birth and death of several generations of ancestors in the New
World was evidently not sufficient reason for considering the Americas
to be the center of their world. Hence the evocation of the primal
moment of separation from Africa as ushering in an extended period
of homelessness:

Por el camino de la mar,

61

con el jazmín y con el toro,
y con la harina y con el hierro,
el negro, para fabricar
el oro;
para llorar en su destierro
por el camino de la mar.

¿Cómo vais a olvidar
lo que las nubes aún pueden recordar?

[Over the path of the sea,
with the jasmine and the bull,
and with flour and with iron,
the black man, to make
gold;
to weep in his exile
over the path of the sea.

How are you going to forget
what the clouds can still remember?]

("Elegía," 1: 239)

As its human subject becomes linked with animals and inanimate objects, the poem reflects on the syntactic level the process of "thingification"[2] into which the African was felt to have been inserted once he had left the security of his ancestral culture. Isolated from the cultural matrix that would render him unmistakably Yoruba or Mandinka even in situations of political and economic oppression, the Afro-American ceased to be recognized as a member of a specific culture and began to be identified by his most visible characteristic, his skin color. From the social being who was Dahomean or Kongo, a purely racial essence was created. Moreover, in crossing the Atlantic, the African was further denuded of his humanity because he was viewed only in economic terms, as sheer labor power. Consequently, the departure from Africa was seen as the falling away from a more harmonious form of existence because of the obligation to assume the role of "fuel-man"[3] in the Americas. Since the wealth created by the African's labor enriched neither him nor the members of his ethnic group, the voyage to the Americas became, in retrospect, simply an occasion for lament.

It is the privileged position of the Spaniard in the New World that causes the black man's hopelessness to appear so absolute. The very seas that launched the European on the path of freedom, by virtue of his capacity to act, thrust the African into a state of unfreedom. Unlike the Afro-American, who was reduced to expressing his "nostalgia for the true human condition,"[4] the *conquistador* was the epitome of assertiveness in that he enlisted religious and secular aid to establish his pattern of dominance in the Americas:

Por el camino de la mar
vino el pirata,
mensajero del Espíritu Malo,
con su cara de un solo mirar
y con su monótona pata
de palo.
Por el camino de la mar.

Hay que aprender a recordar
lo que las nubes no pueden olvidar.
. . . .

Por el camino de la mar,
el pergamino de la ley,
la vara para malmedir,
y el látigo de castigar,
y la sífilis del virrey,
y la muerte, para dormir
sin despertar,
por el camino de la mar.

[Over the path of the sea
came the pirate,
messenger of the Evil Spirit,
with his one-eyed face
and his monotonous wooden
leg.
Over the path of the sea.

One must learn to remember
what the clouds cannot forget.
. . . .

Over the path of the sea,
the parchment of the law,
the rod for measuring falsely,
and the whip for punishing,
and the viceroy's syphilis,
and death, for sleeping
without awakening,
over the path of the sea.]

(1: 239–40)

The false attributes of the pirate and the distorting instruments used by his compatriots to maintain their authority are intended to convey the element of inauthenticity at the heart of the colonial enterprise, inasmuch as the stated intentions of the Europeans were often belied by their actual deeds. Guillén's displacement of the source of agency in the second of the verses cited above also suggests that the institutional forms through which the Europeans supplemented their presence in the Americas came to supply a more lasting equivalent of that presence, by obliterating the traces of the individuals initially responsible for their diffusion, while perpetuating European hegemony. The conscious self of the individual European is subordinated to the collective project of restructuring the American continent and incorporating it within the European frame of reference.[5]

But if religious, legal, administrative, and economic sanctions, as well as diseases and brute force enabled the Europeans to assert their supremacy in the sixteenth century, custom apparently explains their continued dominance in the twentieth-century Caribbean. Centuries of subordination appear to have conditioned blacks to accept as "natural" their obligation to perform the most arduous tasks in their society. Thus, in the following scene, the French need not resort to the whip or to political manipulation to ensure their privileged form of existence, since the docile attitude of the Guadeloupean dockworkers constitutes a tacit endorsement of the principle of the racial division of labor first introduced at the moment of the Conquest:

> Los negros, trabajando
> junto al vapor. Los árabes, vendiendo,
> los franceses, paseando y descansando,
> y el sol, ardiendo.
>
> En el puerto se acuesta
> el mar. El aire tuesta
> las palmeras . . .Yo grito: ¡Guadalupe!, pero nadie contesta.
>
> Parte el vapor, arando
> las aguas impasibles con espumoso estruendo.
> Allá, quedan los negros trabajando,
> los árabes vendiendo,
> los franceses paseando y descansando,
> y el sol ardiendo . . .
>
> [The blacks, working
> beside the ship. The Arabs, selling,
> the French, strolling and resting,
> and the sun, shining.
>
> In the harbor, the sea
> reaches the shore-line. The air burns
> the palm trees . . .I shout: "Guadeloupe!", but nobody answers.
>
> The ship sails, ploughing
> the impassive waters with frothy din.
> There the blacks remain working,
> the Arabs selling,

the French strolling and resting,
and the sun shining . . .]

("Guadalupe W.I.," 1: 171)

The cyclical structure of Guillén's poem points to the immutable character that a historical situation assumed once there was unquestioning
acceptance of the premises upon which it was founded. The lack of
response to the persona's attempt to create an awareness of the eternal
sameness of conditions in Guadeloupe indicates the general acquies-
cence in the continuity of ancient sociopolitical differences.

The unchallenged centrality of the French in Guadeloupe was paral-
leled in pre-Independence Jamaica where the British dominated. Once
they have adopted the symbols of British political culture as their own,
Jamaicans apparently are never in doubt as to their equality of citizenship within the Empire:

> Bajo el hambriento sol
> (God save the King)
> negra de bata blanca
> cantando una canción.
> (God save the King.)
> Una canción.
> ¿Por siempre?
> ¿Por siempre esa canción?
> Oh yes!
> Oh no!
> Oh yes!
>
> Oh no!
>
> [Beneath the hungry sun
> (God save the King)
> a black woman in a white robe
> singing a song.
> (God save the King.)
> A song.
> Forever?
> That song forever?
> Oh yes!
> Oh no!
> Oh yes!
>
> Oh no!]

("Ciudades," 2: 34)

Yet, if for the persona the question of "Britishness" is never at issue, the fact that its expression is confined to the singing of the national anthem indicates that her assumed identity is conceived abstractly in terms of an "absent paradigm"[6] instead of being based on a recognition of her actual characteristics. Having learned to perceive her situation through the mediation of a universalist myth, she remains oblivious to her own circumstances: they do not filter through into her consciousness so as to produce an awareness of her unequal status. Even as the anthem suggests the persona's belief in her identity as a British subject, it is her differentness from the European ideal that she espouses that is immediately brought into focus. Guillén's ironic juxtaposition of the persona's white clothing and black skin is intended to portray the sense of dislocation involved in her acceptance of the political identity imposed upon her by the British, since it necessarily implies a willingness to negate her own manner of being. Unswerving loyalty to a distant metropolis creates emotional distance from Jamaica, which explains the high degree of disinterest in the persona's immediate situation. Guillén's character therefore bears the classic marks of colonization defined by George Lamming, particularly insofar as her desire for self-improvement has been arrested by years of submission to European dominance.[7] The English words interspersed in Guillén's Spanish text call further attention to the devaluation of self entailed by the West Indian's assumption of the language and cultural orientation of her colonizers. If total identification with an alien system of authority is politically advisable in situations of absolute inequality, such as that on which the colonial relationship is grounded, it is also generated by the feeling that one is inessential and contingent.

To judge by his presentation of the state of affairs in Guadeloupe and Jamaica, Guillén apparently perceives a connection between the material deprivation of blacks and the political status of their countries of residence. In other words, there is seemingly a direct relationship between the dependence of Guadeloupe on Europe and the marginal position of Guadeloupe's blacks as compared with the Frenchmen who live on the island. That the subordination of blacks in their own homeland is not necessarily related to the question of direct European rule is patently clear in "Barlovento" (Venezuela) where the signs of hunger and misery are even more apparent than in Jamaica:

El mismo canto
y el mismo cuento,
bajo la luna
de Barlovento.

Negro con hambre,
piernas de soga,
brazos de alambre.

Negro en camisa,
tuberculosis
color ceniza.

Negro en su casa,
cama en el suelo,
fogón sin brasa.

. . . .

Suena, guitarra
de Barlovento,
que lo que digas
lo lleva el viento.

—Dorón dorando,
un negro canta,
y está llorando.

[The same song
and the same story,
beneath the moon
of Barlovento.

Hungry black man,
rope-like legs,
wire-like arms.

A black man in a shirt,
tuberculosis,
ashen color.

A black man at home,
the floor for a bed,
a stove without coals.

. . . .

Play, guitar
from Barlovento,
for whatever you say,
the wind carries away.

"Tra-la, tra-la-la,"
a black man sings,
and he is weeping.]

                                        ("Barlovento," 1: 243-44)

Even though the situation described here is an intranational rather than
an international one, the position of the character in republican Vene-

zuela is structurally similar to that of the Guadeloupean with regard to the Frenchman. In both instances, the disadvantages of the Afro-American are as much a factor of his political and economic circumstances as of his racial and cultural difference. Hence the term "internal colonialism" is often applied to cases like Venezuela, where the national system of social stratification makes for visibility of status, since it is based on the same ascriptive criteria first used by Europeans for transfixing the people of Africa, Latin America, and the Caribbean within their respective empires.[8]

Given the degraded conditions in which he was forced to live, the Afro-Venezuelan evidently sought to retain his humanity by investing his creative energies in art forms that expressed his actual situation, which also bore the traces of a reconstituted ethnic heritage. In René Depestre's terms, this became a form of "cultural maroonage," inasmuch as it represented a refusal to accept as definitive the experience of the Middle Passage, by which Africans came to be inserted to their disadvantage in a new sociopolitical order in the Americas.[9] Yet while music and oral history served to maintain the Afro-Venezuelan's sense of community, they also reinforced the tendency to regard him as a separate sociocultural entity. Since his artistic contributions went unrecognized as such, they were made to appear ephemeral and to have little import in the shaping of the national culture. Moreover, the elegiac tone of the Afro-Venezuelan's music heightens the sense of his separateness from a living tradition. The static images of the persona, marked by the absence of verbs in Guillén's text, would therefore correspond to the Afro-Venezuelan's isolation in a timeless world—a world in which change is absent.

The abject condition of Afro-Americans in the twentieth century results from the cumulative effect of social practices that were once underwritten by colonial law. Despite the scholarly claims made for the benevolent attitude of the Spaniards toward their racially different colonial subjects, by virtue of the humanitarian ideals expressed in decrees periodically issued from the metropolis,[10] the fact is that those who were entrusted with implementing such decrees were an ocean away from the source that issued them, and these administrators were less attentive to abstract statements on the God-given dignity of all human beings than they were to the political and socioeconomic reality of maintaining jurisdiction over a people who were perceived primarily as problems that had to be regulated. Furthermore, colonial laws were themselves discriminatory in that they permitted justice to be rendered differentially on the grounds of race:

Según uso e costumbre,
en reunión del Cabildo fue acordado:
Que las sendas que salen de la playa
se cierren e no haya
habitante ninguno tan osado
de las abrir, pues ha llegado aviso
de que este pueblo e villa
recuestado e robado
de piratas franceses
fue, e que por más de un punto penetraron;
si es español, so pena
de que pague mil pesos
para gastos de guerra,
o recibir azotes hasta cien
si acaso desta plata careciera;
si negra libre fuera,
o mulata tal vez o mero esclavo,
que sea desjarretado
de un pie; si fuese indio, que trabaje
en la obra del Fuerte un año entero.

[*According to use and custom,*
at a meeting of the town council it was decided:
That the paths leading from the beach
should be closed and that
no citizen should dare
to open them, since news has arrived
that this town and city
has been attacked and robbed
by French pirates
and that they entered through more than one place;
if he is a Spaniard, under penalty
of paying one thousand pesos
for war expenses,
or receiving up to one hundred lashes
if he happens to lack this money;
if it should be a free Negress,
or a mulatto woman, by chance, or simply a slave,
he should be hamstrung
in one foot; if he is an Indian, let him work
for one whole year on the construction of the Fort.]

("Pregón segundo," 2: 375)

The various social categories mentioned in Guillén's poem indicate that in a racially mixed slave society, which Cuba had become by the early sixteenth century,[11] both the degree of racial mixture and the condition of being free were important in determining one's social status. However, in times of real or imagined emergency, these distinctions were superseded by the more basic polarization between Europeans and non-

Europeans.[12] The questionable nature of the Spaniards' commitment to socioracial equality is revealed by the ease with which racial discontinuity was reaffirmed.

Nevertheless, Guillén's reference to the superior status of the Spaniard acts as a reminder that in colonial society, American-born whites were also less equal than Europeans. Admittedly, unlike Indians and Africans, *criollos,* whose physical appearance did not serve as a mark of their presumed deviation from the standards of biological perfection, were permitted to engage in a wider range of economic activities than were the darker groups. However, until the beginning of the twentieth century, *criollos,* like all other Cubans, were excluded from participation in the political affairs of their country. Such matters as the need for security and relations with the outside world were determined by the representatives of the mother country.

Consequently, from Guillén's point of view, when the socioracial cleavages of the colonial past are set against the heritage of political inequality shared by all Cubans, it is the latter disability that assumes greater significance. Thus, in the following poem, disparity of social origins is mentioned only to be negated dramatically in the final lines of the monologue:

> Por lo que dices, Fabio,
> un arcángel tu abuelo fue con sus esclavos.
> Mi abuelo, en cambio,
> fue un diablo con sus amos.
> El tuyo murió de un garrotazo.
> Al mío, lo colgaron.

> [From what you say, Fabio,
> your grandfather was an archangel with his slaves.
> My grandfather, on the other hand,
> was a devil with his masters.
> Yours was executed.
> They hanged mine.]

("Ancestros," 2: 285)

In both instances, the actions ascribed to the prototypical ancestor—the master who seeks to mask his domination, the slave who attempts to refuse his condition—are an explicit challenge to the colonial system of hierarchical relationships. The paradoxical attributes with which the two grandfathers are endowed—the master who should have been a devil but was an "archangel," the slave who should have been an archangel but was a "devil"—suggest the irreconcilable conflicts generated by their unorthodox behavior. At the same time, the rhetoric of theology from which the metaphors of polarity are derived heightens the intensity of the social tensions represented by placing them beyond the realm of human relations. In a plantation society committed to maintaining rigid distinctions between yours/mine, master/slave, archangel/devil, any attempt to blur these distinctions is perceived as a threat to social equilibrium and is necessarily punished by death. However, for the speaking subject, it is this very desire for apartness that allows him to establish a common ground of experience with his hypothetical listener, as evidenced by the similar fate attributed to their respective grandfathers. The evocation of the polar categories of the past is therefore informed by the antithetical impulse to transcend them.

What is initially perceived in Guillén's poem to be separate attempts on the part of individuals from opposite ends of the social spectrum to undermine the colonial order was, in effect, a joint project by Afro-Cubans and *criollos* to achieve political emancipation for all Cubans.[13] But if the long struggle for independence ultimately meant the severing of political ties with Spain, it did not signal the end of European dominance. In artistic matters, Paris remained the undisputed center:

El inocente indígena,
el decorado artista provincial
recién París, recién
Barrio Latino y tantas cosas
como la muchachita rubia,
el vino y la miseria,
está ni alumno ni maestro.

Pinta días en rosa.
Con el cincel desbasta (eso piensa) el futuro.
Con la pluma bordea imitaciones.
Discute a gritos,
discute a gritos de alba en alba
junto al zinc del bistrot,
de Modigliani y de Picasso,
de Verlaine, de Rimbaud.

Y América esperando.

[The innocent native,
the decorated provincial artist
new to Paris, new
in the Latin Quarter and to so many things
like the blond girl,
wine and poverty,
is neither a student nor a teacher.

He paints days in pink.
With his chisel he shapes (that's what he thinks) the future.

With his pen he borders imitations.
He argues loudly,
he argues loudly from one dawn to the next
near the galvanized iron roof of the bistro,
about Modigliani and Picasso,
about Verlaine, about Rimbaud.

And America, still waiting.]

("París," 2: 290-91)

Guillén's "native" exemplifies the long line of Latin American artists who have been accustomed to seeing their own landscape through alien eyes.[14] Ever since the Conquest, when the irruption of European conquerors into Latin America led to European control of the major aspects of life, local forms of expression tended to be mediated by the European presence. At first, metropolitan approval was essential for survival in view of the fact that the ships that carried viceroys and sugar mills also brought food for the body and for the mind. And since the facilities of the mother country enabled the artist's work to reach a much wider audience than was available in his own country, the artist who sought to distinguish himself among his peers often felt obliged to situate himself in the metropolitan center. Eventually, what might once have been a logical necessity merged with cultural alienation, and the voyage to Europe in itself began to be regarded as an index of artistic excellence.

For Guillén's character, the customary trip to Paris appears to have been warranted by his isolation from a stimulating cultural environment. However, in this instance, the benefits to be derived from exposure to another world are immediately nullified by the encroachment of that other world on the original one. The character is revealed to be a prisoner of the idea that others have of artistic invention. In his anxiety not to appear out-of-date, he meticulously sets about reproducing European techniques without realizing that they are anterior to his notion of the avant-garde. Whether he functions as painter, sculptor, or writer, to Guillén's artist, the facile deployment of preexisting elements of form takes precedence over the careful elaboration of appropriate modes of self-expression. Hence he exudes an aspect of in-betweenness since his work is not anchored to a specific vision of its relationship to his world, but instead has become purely decorative and divorced from the environment that it claims to represent. As if verbal appropriation were to be equated with creativity, the names of European artists are abstracted from their milieu and made to serve as authoritative sources in a dizzying round of conversations where stridency of tone is expected to will into being the originality that should have been achieved through introspection. The indiscriminate accumulation of ready-made points of reference represents a will to synthesis, which has been cited by Fanon as a sign of the colonized, inasmuch as it is expressed in the condensation of successive stages of another's experiences and in uncritical attempts to appropriate those experiences without first questioning their suitability to the subject's internal needs.[15] Thus, what should have given rise to an increasing mastery of expressive techniques results in a dispersal of creative energies. Yet, Guillén's artist is incapable of recognizing the superfluous character of his own productions. Having set the necessity of catching up with others over and above the articulation of a vision appropriate to the present moment, the artist deceives himself as to the limiting effect of his over-reliance on precedents on his creative output. Since his work is oriented neither to his current place of residence nor to the scene of his professional reputation, he remains immobilized in a cultural void.

Just as "París" suggests the lack of congruence between the political status of a country and its degree of cultural autonomy, other poems indicate that a republican constitution was no guarantee of economic independence. The monopoly previously exercised by the Spaniards over the principal segments of Cuba's economy came to be enjoyed by North Americans who not only failed to diversify the island's economic activity but also continued the previous pattern of the racial division of labor:

> El negro
> junto al cañaveral.
>
> El yanqui
> sobre el cañaveral.
>
> La tierra
> bajo el cañaveral.
>
> ¡Sangre
> que se nos va!
>
> [The black man
> beside the canefield.
>
> The American
> over the canefield.
>
> The land
> beneath the canefield.
>
> Blood
> that is draining away from us!]

> ("Caña," 1: 129)

Admittedly, until the middle of the twentieth century, a substantial portion of the island was devoted to the cultivation of other crops. But the central place of sugar in the economy and the use of the best land for the growing of sugar cane[16] created the sense of the island's being a vast canefield, as signified by the obsessive recurrence of the word, "canefield," in Guillén's poem. The inversion of the usual relationship between the land and its products, with the land being situated "under the canefield" instead of the canefield being placed "on it,"[17] suggests the total subordination of Cuba's cultivable area to the tyranny of the canefield. While relationships to the canefield would change over the years, the monotonous presence of the canefield would remain a constant in the Cuban landscape.

By the same token, a considerable amount of the sugar-producing areas was still in Cuban hands at the beginning of the twentieth century.[18] However, Cuban inability to compete with the harvests of American-owned lands, the fact that most refineries were located in the United States, and American control of the processes of milling, shipping, and marketing,[19] all generated the feeling that the canefields were completely subordinated to the will of the United States. Since sugar was itself the island's primary source of income, American control of the sugar industry is likened to the draining away of the nation's lifeblood.

That Cuba's land and labor were made to serve interests other than her own was not the only consequence of American ownership of many canefields. A more immediate result was the curtailment of the existential possibilities of the population, due to the inefficient patterns of land use represented by the sugar plantation.[20] The continued focus on the commercial production of a single crop for export rather than on growing food for local consumption resulted in social and economic stagnation:

> El hombre de tierra adentro
> está en un hoyo metido,
> muerto sin haber nacido,
> el hombre de tierra adentro.
> Y el hombre de la ciudad,
> ay, Cuba, es un pordiosero:
> anda hambriento y sin dinero,
> pidiendo por caridad,
> aunque se ponga sombrero
> y baile en la sociedad.
> (Lo digo en mi son entero,
> porque es la pura verdad.)
>
> Hoy yanqui, ayer española,
> sí, señor,

la tierra que nos tocó,
siempre el pobre la encontró
si hoy yanqui, ayer española,
¡cómo no!
¡Qué sola la tierra sola,
la tierra que nos tocó!

[The man from the countryside
is stuck in a hole,
dead without having been born,
the man from the countryside.
And the man from the city,
oh, Cuba, is a beggar:
he walks around hungry and penniless,
begging for charity,
although he might wear a hat
and dance in society.
(I say it in my complete ballads,
because it is the plain truth.)

Today American, yesterday Spanish,
yes sir,
the land which is ours,
some wretch always found it
because today American, yesterday Spanish,
of course!
How desolate the desolate land,
the land which is ours!]

("Mi patria es dulce por fuera. . . ," 1: 226)

The signs of decay were most evident in the countryside, since the city, by virtue of its closer links with the metropolitan economy, succeeded in masking its poverty to a greater extent.[21]

Moreover, the substantial investment that the ownership of Cuban canefields and sugar mills represented for American financial interests eventually necessitated the protection of troops to guard it from attack in times of labor unrest. The formation of an army, whose primary function came to be the suppression of labor disputes so as to ensure the smooth functioning of the sugar harvest, gave it the character of "an army of occupation" in the eyes of the local population[22] and heightened the sense of displacement already aroused by American ownership of Cuban property:

¡Ah de los trenes de tropas,
fríos al amanecer,
en duros rieles de sangre
corriendo a todo correr,
para aplastar una huelga

o estrangular un batey!
Soldado así no he de ser.

. . . .

Soldado así quiero ser.
El que no cuida el central,
que no es dél,
ni reina, como un rey tosco
de cuartel,
ni sobre el campo de caña
tiras arranca de piel,
feroz igual que un negrero,
y aún más cruel.

[Alas! The trains with troops,
cold at daybreak,
on hard rails of blood,
running with all speed
to crush a strike
or to stifle a peasant's plot!
That kind of soldier I do not have to be.

. . . .

This kind of soldier I am supposed to be.
He who does not watch over the sugar refinery,
which is not his,
nor reigns, like a coarse
barracks king,
nor on the cane field
tears off strips of skin,
fierce just like a slave trader,
and even more cruel.]

("Soldado así no he de ser," 1: 183-84)

The unfavorable comparison of the soldier's brutality to the behavior of the slave trader indicates the degree to which the army was regarded as the agent of indirect American rule.

At the same time, the conditions under which Cuba was granted independence from Spain led, on occasion, to the presence of American warships in Cuban territorial waters and/or the landing of American troops on Cuban soil. One of the results of the entry of the United States into Cuba's Second War of Independence, ostensibly as Cuba's ally, but primarily to defend American economic interests against further destruction by the warring forces, was that the United States was present when Cuba became a republic. It is not surprising, therefore, that the United States should have been granted the legal right to intervene in Cuban affairs whenever political stability was felt to be threatened.[23] The climate of uncertainty created by confrontations between dissatisfied elements and the incumbent government during the early republican years led to extended periods of military intervention by the United States.[24] It is the compromise of sovereignty represented by such interventions that Guillén deplores in the following lines:

Cuba, palmar vendido,
sueño descuartizado,
duro mapa de azúcar y de olvido . . .
. . . .

Afuera está el vecino.
Tiene el teléfono y el submarino.
Tiene una flota bárbara, una flota
bárbara. . . . Tiene una montaña de oro
y un mirador y un coro
de águilas y una nube de soldados
ciegos, sordos, armados
por el miedo y el odio. (Sus banderas
empastadas en sangre, un fisiológico
hedor esparcen que demora el vuelo
de las moscas.) Afuera está el vecino,
rodeado de fieras
nocturnas, enviando embajadores,
. . . .

y también desde luego,
tropas de infantería de marina,
porque es útil (a veces) hacer fuego . . .

[Cuba, sold-out palm field,
dismembered dream,
hard map of sugar and oblivion . . .
. . . .

The neighbor is outside.
He has the telephone and the submarine.
He has a barbarous fleet, a barbarous
fleet. . . He has a mountain of gold
and a belvedere and a chorus
of eagles and a cloud of soldiers,
blind, deaf, armed
through fear and hatred. (His flags
plastered with blood, spread a physiological
stench which delays the flight
of flies.) The neighbor is outside,
surrounded by nocturnal
fiends, sending ambassadors,
. . . .

and of course,
troops from the marine corps also,
because it is useful (sometimes) to shoot . . .]

("Elegía cubana," 1: 389–92)

Through the techniques of repetition and accumulation, the poet suggests the virtually unlimited aggressive capability that the United States could deploy against a defenseless Cuba, a Cuba armed only with its "palm trees" and its "sugar."

Obviously, the presence of American forces in Cuba was not simply a problem of territoriality. It also signified the occupation of one country by another, which showed lack of due respect for the meaningful symbols of the local culture. Serious misunderstandings arose when the two ethnic groups, with their different expectations, met:

> Son los sucios marines borrachos que caminan
> con zapatos de estiércol sobre bestiales rutas
> y en la sagrada frente de los héroes orinan
> y ven en nuestras hijas nocturnas prostitutas.

> [They are the dirty, drunken marines who walk
> with dung-covered shoes upon beastly routes
> and urinate on the sacred brow of the heroes
> and see our daughters as sad prostitutes.]

("Frente al Oxford," 2: 87)

The poet's resentment at the affront to national dignity that the actions of the marines constituted[25] is conveyed by the rhetorical siting of the national monuments in a realm of untouchability and the corresponding reduction of the marines to a subhuman level.

Nevertheless, if American contempt for Cuba's culture provoked a sense of outrage, the loss of life resulting from each occupation aroused the desire for a violent reversal:

> Otra vez Peralejo
> bien pudiera marcar con dura llama
> no la piel del león domado y viejo,
> sino el ala del pájaro sangriento
> que desde el alto Norte desparrama
> muerte, gusano y muerte, cruz y muerte,
> lágrima y muerte, muerte y sepultura,
> muerte y microbio, muerte y bayoneta,
> muerte y estribo, muerte y herradura,
> muerte de arma secreta,
> muerte del muerto herido solitario,
> muerte del joven de verde corona,
> muerte del inocente campanario;
> muerte previa, prevista,
> ensayada en Las Vegas,
> con aviones a chorro y bombas ciegas.

> [Once again Peralejo
> could well brand with harsh flames

not the pelt of the old and tamed lion,
but the wing of the bloodthirsty bird
that from the lofty North spreads
death, worms and death, a cross and death,
tears and death, death and burials,
death and microbes, death and the bayonet,
death and the stirrup, death and a horseshoe,
death by secret weapon,
death of the lonely, wounded man,
death of the youth with the green crown,
death of the innocent belfry;
preliminary, anticipated death,
rehearsed in Las Vegas,
with jet planes and blind bombs.]

("Elegía cubana," 1: 393)

Yet, with the very yearning for another battle of Peralejo, there comes a recognition of Cuba's altered circumstances. Temporal distance has subdued the hostility once directed at Spain, which is now perceived to be exhausted and defeated, while the proximity of the American military presence explains the intensity of the poet's denunciations of the United States. The recurrence of "death" in the catalogue of accusations for which retribution is sought indicates that the United States is felt to be far more threatening to Cuban existence than Spain ever was. At the same time, the potential mode in which the enunciation is cast, and the hyperbolic manner in which the enumeration of charges is stated, point to an underlying sense of despair at the prospect of a definitive rupture with the United States. The soaring eagle appears to be beyond the range of having its wings clipped, whereas the "lion," before it was "tamed," was not.

Perhaps the frustration evident in the lines cited above stems from Guillén's awareness that the decision on American intervention in Cuban affairs was not necessarily unilateral. For once Cuba had been established as a republic and the forces of the first American occupation had withdrawn, it was the opposition parties on the island who sought, or invoked the threat of, American intervention as a means of contesting unfavorable election results. Since the elected government itself had often come into being through the mediation of the United States, the concept of representative government remained a constitutional ideal during the early republican years.[26]

That the relationship of politicians to their constituents was a mediated one is demonstrated by the following verses:

—Coroneles de terracota,
políticos de quita y pon;

café con pan y mantequilla . . .
¡Que siga el son!

La burocracia está de acuerdo
en ofrendarse a la Nación;
doscientos dólares mensuales . . .
¡Que siga el son!

El yanqui nos dará dinero
para arreglar la situación;
la Patria está por sobre todo . . .
¡Que siga el son!

Los viejos líderes sonríen
y hablan después desde un balcón.
¡La zafra! ¡La zafra! ¡La zafra!
¡Que siga el son!

["Terracotta colonels,
removable politicians;
coffee with bread and butter . . .
Let the ballad go on!

The bureaucracy is agreed
to contribute to the Nation;
two hundred dollars monthly . . .
Let the ballad go on!

The Yankee will give us money
to fix the situation;
The Fatherland comes before everything . . .
Let the ballad go on!

The old leaders smile
and speak afterwards from a balcony.
The harvest! The harvest! The harvest!
Let the ballad go on!"]

("West Indies, Ltd.," 1: 161)

For it was obvious that the center of power lay elsewhere. Despite the rhetoric of nationalism, the "terracotta colonels" and "removable politicians" were evidently committed to no philosophy of government except that of satisfying their immediate self-interest. The "fatherland" thus came to be perceived simply as an analogous version of the self.[27] And "service" to self and society was rendered through the financial aid of the United States. The patriotic ideals expressed in public statements therefore served only as a ritualistic mask for political insubstantiality. Even as politicians extolled the virtues of patriotism in their speeches, they were draining those speeches of referential significance by their willingness to assume a secondary role to the United States in the resolution of the nation's problems. Rhetorical appeals to their constituents were necessary for maintaining the appearance of legitimacy.

But prior accountability to the United States rather than to internal forces signified their complicity in their own subordination.

The gap between public statements and political practice was often a result of pressures applied directly by the United States. Since Cuba was considered to be strategically and economically important to the United States, the freedom of local politicians tended to be circumscribed by the American ambassador, who was generally entrusted with securing the implementation of policies favorable to American interests:

> Es el embajador en camisa que ordena
> con el garrote en alto la rendición sumisa,
> y el yes y el very good y el okéi . . . La cadena
> que sofoca el resuello y estrangula la risa.
>
> [It is the ambassador in shirt sleeves who orders
> submissive surrender with the big stick raised,
> and the yes and very good and the okay . . . The chain
> which stifles breathing and strangles laughter.]

("Frente al Oxford," 2: 87)

Admittedly, the nature of the role varied over the years according to the political climate in the United States and the temperament of the individual ambassador. What remained essentially unchanged until 1959 was the decisive influence of the American embassy in the shaping of Cuban "national" policy.[28]

Given the second-order role assumed by Cuban politicians in the making of their own history, it is not surprising that the island over which they "ruled" should have been engulfed by the products of American consumer culture:

> Aquí están los servidores de Mr. Babbit.
> Los que educan sus hijos en West Point.
> Aquí están los que chillan: hello baby,
> y fuman "Chesterfield" y "Lucky Strike."
> Aquí están los bailadores de fox trots,
> los boys del jazz band
> y los veraneantes de Miami y de Palm Beach.
> Aquí están los que piden bread and butter
> y coffee and milk.
>
> [Here are the servants of Mr. Babbitt.
> Those who educate their sons at West Point.
> Here are those who scream: hello baby,
> and smoke "Chesterfield" and "Lucky Strike."
> Here are the dancers of fox trots,
> the boys of the jazz band
> and the summer vacationers in Miami and Palm Beach.
> Here are those who ask for bread and butter
> and coffee and milk.]

("West Indies, Ltd.," 1: 166)

From the point of view of the marketers of these commodities, Cuba was simply being provided with items that the island was incapable of producing for itself. However, when one recalls that the island was a supplier of one of the world's finest varieties of tobacco and was at the same time purchasing a processed version of the product in the form of "Chesterfield" and "Lucky Strike," the unequal structure of the economic exchange becomes evident. Through aggressive advertising campaigns, Cubans were made to luxuriate in the pleasures of unbalancing the national budget for the greater financial happiness of American cigarette manufacturers.

Besides, as Guillén's poem indicates, it was not only commodities that were introduced onto the island. Dancing the fox trot became highly desirable, and other dance forms, including the rumba, were downgraded. The proliferation of English words, strategically located in a syntactic position of emphasis in Guillén's text, expresses the disruption that adopting American patterns of consumption caused for the Cuban. It was not only excessive materialism that posed a threat to the Cuban self, as Guillén's reference to "Mr. Babbitt" seems to imply.[29] The availability of American goods also initiated a substitutive movement that deflected attention from the local scene and oriented it toward the continental center of production. As Cubans were made to experience the need for certain services, they also acquired the supplementary desire to articulate their preferences in the idiom of the American producers. Since English was adopted as a substitute for, rather than an addition to, Cuban Spanish, the use of English phrases represented a discontinuity with the self.

The similarity of products available to both Cubans and Americans created an illusion of sameness and gave Cubans the impression that, through functional analogy, they were installed in the productive center. The project of self-realization was thereby deferred in an attempt to suppress the difference between the Cuban self and the American other. Hence, the fetishistic use of American commodities as status symbols, whose pervasiveness is suggested by the anaphora, "here are . . ." At the same time, the linguistic dislocation in the lines cited above reflects the suspended status of the Cuban quest for a borrowed identity. If Palm Beach could dislodge Varadero as the ideal vacation spot, other existential factors proved more resilient to the tendency toward homogenizing Cuban and American experience. The limited repertoire of verbal signs manipulated by certain Cubans only served to indicate the distance separating them from their American equivalents, and thus came to register the frustration of a desire for parity based on the criterion of exteriority. Instead of constituting an affirmation of equality, mimetic behavior could express only a diminished mode of being.

The constricting of the dimensions of the Cuban self was not only embodied linguistically but was also reflected in terms of spatial relationships. If the commercial presence of the United States signified a retreat from the sounds of Cuban Spanish, the physical presence of American tourists dispelled the sense of the island being a place of residence. Instead, it acquired a superfluous identity as a playground existing for the sole purpose of entertaining world-weary travellers:

> ¡Ah, tierra insular!
> ¡Ah, tierra estrecha!
> ¿No es cierto que parece hecha
> sólo para poner un palmar?
> Tierra en la ruta del "Orinoco",
> o de otro barco excursionista,
> repleto de gente sin un artista
> y sin un loco;
> puertos donde el que regresa de Tahití,
> de Afganistán o de Seúl,
> viene a comerse el cielo azul,
> regándolo con Bacardí;
> puertos que hablan un inglés
> que empieza en yes y acaba en yes.
> (Inglés de cicerones en cuatro pies.)

> [Ah, insular land!
> Ah, narrow land!
> Isn't it true that you seem to be created
> only for the placing of a palm grove?
> Land on the route of the "Orinoco,"
> or of some other cruise ship,
> filled with people without an artist
> and without a fool;
> ports where he who is on his way from Tahiti,
> from Afghanistan or from Seoul,
> comes to enjoy the blue sky,
> watering it with Bacardi;
> ports which speak an English
> that begins with yes and ends with yes.
> (The English of tour guides on all fours.)]

(1: 159-60)

Guillén's consciousness of the degraded status of the island is expressed in the lament for another image of the Cuban landscape. Hence, the very elements that ordinarily are depicted as indispensable to the idyllic scenery of tourist brochures—palm trees, blue sky, sea, and rum—are perceived with a sense of estrangement, since they seem to have been intended only for the enjoyment of others. Far from representing the creative use of the island's natural resources, as tourism is usually portrayed by its official promoters, in Guillén's view, tourism is contrary to the national interest since it is the leisure aspect for others that assumes primacy rather than the ostensible benefits that can be gained by the national treasury.

Moreover, tourism is deplored as demeaning to the island's integrity, since being invested with the character of a vacation resort means living up to its projected image of hedonism:[30]

> Noches pobladas de prostitutas,
> bares poblados de marineros;
> encrucijada de cien rutas
> para bandidos y bucaneros.
> Cuevas de vendedores de morfina,
> de cocaína y de heroína.
> Cabarets donde el tedio se engaña
> con el ilusorio cordial
> de una botella de champaña,
> en cuya eficacia la gente confía
> como en un neosalvarsán de alegría
> para la "sífilis sentimental".
> Ansia de penetrar el porvenir
> y sacar de su entraña secreta
> una fórmula concreta
> para vivir.
> Furor de los piratas de levita
> que como en Sores y "El Olonés",
> frente a la miseria se irrita
> y se resuelve en puntapiés.
>
> [Nights full of prostitutes,
> bars filled with sailors;
> crossroads of one hundred routes
> for bandits and buccaneers.
> Dens of venders of morphine,
> of cocaine and heroin.
> Cabarets where boredom is warded off
> with the illusory cordial
> of a bottle of champagne,
> on whose efficacy people rely
> as if it were a potion of joy
> for "sentimental syphilis."
> Anxiety to see into the future
> and to extract from its secret heart
> a concrete formula
> for living.
> Fury of the white-collar pirates
> who, as in Sores and "El Olonés,"
> when faced with poverty, become irritated
> and resolve it with kicks.]

(1: 163-64)

The atmosphere of decadence and sensuality barely conceals the pain and despair on the other side of the glitter. Indeed, in Lemuel Johnson's terms, "the tropical *paradiso* has become an *inferno.*"[31] The natural beauty of the landscape has fallen away into the almost legendary underworld of Old Havana, where Guillén's syntax condemns people, time, and places to the same ceaseless round of purposeless activity. Because the demand of the visitors for novelty is insatiable, the islanders are felt to have been separated from an authentic mode of experience by their obligation to entertain others. The island's openness to ships and its closure to its inhabitants therefore give it the dualistic aspect of an "Eden for tourists and hell for Cubans."[32]

Furthermore, American tourists are regarded as an obtrusive presence, since their conspicuous affluence calls attention to the poverty of the local inhabitants:

> Todos estos yanquis rojos
> son hijos de un camarón,
> y los parió una botella,
> una botella de ron.
> ¿Quién los llamó?
> Ustedes viven,
> me muero yo,
> comen y beben,
> pero yo no,
> pero yo no,
> pero yo no.

> [All these ruddy Americans
> are sons of a shrimp,
> and a bottle gave birth to them,
> a bottle of rum.
> Who called you?
> You are alive,
> I am dying,
> you eat and drink,
> but I don't,
> but I don't,
> but I don't.]

> ("Cantaliso en un bar," 1: 201)

Visual awareness of what is empirically inaccessible heightens the persona's sense of marginality, for he is as incapable of improving his material situation as he is of regulating the living advertisements for material success. The proximity of socially mobile Americans therefore serves the dubious purpose of thrusting upon the persona a consciousness of the difference between existential possibility and its negation.

The indignation that the presence of well-fed Americans calls into being is also aroused by American displacement of local initiative in other areas of experience. The parallel perceived between Cuba's lack of autonomy and the frustration of Venezuela's desire for internal development evokes a similar cry of protest:

> —Canto en Cuba y Venezuela,
> y una canción se me sale:
> ¡qué petróleo tan amargo,
> caramba,
> ay, qué amargo este petróleo,
> caramba,
> que a azúcar cubano sabe!
>
> ¡Cante, Juan Bimba,
> yo lo acompaño!
>
> La misma mano extranjera
> que está sobre mi bandera,
> la estoy mirando en La Habana:
> ¡pobre bandera cubana,
> cubana o venezolana,
> con esa mano extranjera,
> inglesa o americana
> mandándonos desde fuera!
>
> ["I sing in Cuba and Venezuela,
> and one song is on my lips:
> what bitter petroleum,
> wow,
> ah, how bitter this petroleum,
> wow,
> that tastes like Cuban sugar!"
>
> Sing, Juan Bimba,
> I will accompany you!
>
> The same foreign hand
> that is on my flag,
> I am seeing it in Havana:
> poor Cuban flag,
> Cuban or Venezuelan,
> with that foreign hand,
> English or American,
> commanding us from without!]
>
> ("Son venezolano," 1: 240-41)

Inasmuch as the focus of Guillén's verses shifts from the flavor of Cuban sugar and Venezuelan oil to the fact of these resources being subordinated to Anglo-American control, the thrust of the argument passes from a simple statement on economic affairs to the outlining of a problem that requires a political solution.

In the following section we shall see how Guillén articulates his perceptions of an alternative political system. Yet, the poet is not simply concerned with the question of Cuban and Venezuelan dependence. By appealing to the bonds of historical experience, he also projects himself as the bearer of a continental consciousness:

monstruo de dos cabezas, mas ninguna con seso,
no importa que nos hable de alianza y de progreso.

Y tal vez porque habla, pues nadie en nuestra América
(india pálida y virgen, pero que no es histérica),

librado ya del férreo dogal de las Españas
va a creer a los yanquis sus tontas musarañas.

. . . .

Para el yanqui no somos más que escoria barata,
tribus de compra fácil con vidrio y hojalata;

generales imbéciles sin ciencia y sin escuela,
ante el jamón colgado cada uno en duermevela;

compadres argentinos, sátrapas peruanos,
betancures, peraltas, muñoces . . . Cuadrumanos

a saltos en la selva; gente menuda y floja
que en curare mortífero sus agrias puntas moja.

Pero como tenemos bosques y cafetales,
hierro, carbón, petróleo, cobre, cañaverales,

(lo que en dólares quiere decir muchos millones),
no importa que seamos quéchuas o motilones.

Vienen pues a ayudarnos para que progresemos
y en pago de su ayuda nuestra sangre les demos.

[monster with two heads, but neither with brains,
never mind that it speaks to us of Alliance and of Progress.

And perhaps because it speaks, since no one in our America
(pale, Indian virgin, but one that is not hysterical),

now freed from the iron yoke of Spain,
is going to believe the Americans' foolish lies.

. . . .

For the American we are only cheap garbage,
tribes easily bribed with glass and tin plate;

feeble-minded generals without knowledge and without education,
each one dozing before a hanging leg of ham;

Argentine strong men, Peruvian satraps,
Betancourts, Peraltas, Muñozes . . . Quadrumanous primates

leaping in the jungle; petty, weak folk
who dip their rough arrowheads in deadly curare.

But since we have forests and coffee plantations,
iron, coal, petroleum, copper, canefields,

(which in dollars means several millions),
it doesn't matter that we are Quechua or Motilones.

So they come to help us to progress
and in payment for their help we give them our blood.]
                              ("Crecen altas las flores," 2: 82–83)

The affirmation of racial and cultural continuity becomes the means by which the differences between Latin Americans and North Americans are established. Cultural polarization becomes a necessary first step in the project of defining a Latin American sense of self, for the appeal to a hemispheric identity is expected to lead to the adoption of a common stance toward the economic exploitation of the continent.

As we shall see, the desire for self-completion led to the call for an end to North American hegemony in the Americas. In the beginning, because of political circumstances, the cry was expressed in the language of virtuality. However, once Cuba underwent its own process of revolutionary transformation, the Cuban experience provided the backdrop against which the need for a new Latin American identity would be defined. What was desired was an end to self-estrangement and the assumption by Latin Americans of the political and economic orientation of their respective countries.

Part Two

TOWARD
A NEW VISION
OF THE
SELF IN SOCIETY

CHAPTER 5

THE
MARXIST
PERSPECTIVE

As we have seen, the referential nature of Guillén's verse meant that his poetry readily became a vehicle for diagnosing the ills of society. At the outset, the focus of Guillén's poetry was on the problems of a marginalized sector of the Cuban population. The poet's realization that Afro-Cubans were embedded in a larger chain of social relationships subsequently led to a broadening of his poetic vision. The *bembón's* self-estrangement, Sabas's poverty, the exploitation of the boxer—all these experiences could now be seen not as merely racially specific conditions but as manifestations of the second-order status of many Cubans during the 1930s. Informing many of the poet's verses that described the way things were was a sense that they ought not to be as they were. Thus, there was a gradual shift in emphasis from the descriptive to the prescriptive. When Guillén embraced the Marxist philosophy in 1937, the normative thrust of his poetry became more pronounced. Because the prevailing political and economic system was recognized to be defective, and because it was thought that social existence determined consciousness,[1] Guillén recommended that the entire social structure be radically altered so as to make possible a qualitative change in the Cuban manner of being.

It was stated in the previous chapter that the dominance of the United States was felt to be a major obstacle in the path of Cuban self-expression. In the following verses, Guillén clearly indicates that authenticity would be facilitated by disengagement from American influence:

De dos en dos,
las maracas se adelantan al yanqui
para decirle:
     —¿Cómo está usted, señor?

91

Cuando hay barco a la vista,
están ya las maracas en el puerto,
vigilando la presa excursionista
con ojo vivo y ademán despierto.
¡Maraca equilibrista,
güiro adulón del dólar del turista!

Pero hay otra maraca con un cierto
pudor que casi es antimperialista:
es la maraca artista,
que no tiene que hacer nada en el puerto.

A ésa le basta con que un negro pobre
la sacuda en el fondo del sexteto:
riñe con el bongó, que es indiscreto,
y el ron que beba es del que al negro sobre.

Ésa ignora que hay yanquis en el mapa;
vive feliz, ralla su pan sonoro,
y el duro muslo a Mamá Inés destapa
y pule y bruñe más la Rumba de oro.

[In pairs,
the maracas rush up to the American
to say to him:
            "How are you, sir?"

When there is a ship in sight,
the maracas are already at the port,
inspecting the tourist prey
with a shrewd eye and alert gestures.
Acrobatic maraca,
gourd grovelling in pursuit of the tourist dollar!

But there is another maraca with a kind of
modesty that is almost anti-imperialist:
it is the artistic maraca,
that is not obliged to do anything at the port.

For that one it is enough that a poor black man
rattles it in the back of the sextet;
it fights with the bongo, which is indiscreet,
and the rum that it drinks comes from the black man's surplus.

That one does not know that there are Americans on the map;
it lives happily, grates its bread loudly,
and reveals the firm thigh of Mamá Inés,
and polishes and further refines the excellent Rumba.]

                                          ("Maracas," 1: 146-47)

Once existence ceased to be mediated by the American presence, it was believed that work would no longer be an alienated activity that was undertaken with a view to pleasing others and motivated solely by the desire for profit. Instead, a change in the conditions of production would presumably lead to a release of creative energies, since human activity would now be freely chosen and would respond to the fulfillment of an inner need.[2] It is also suggested, in the final stanzas of the poem, that when art ceased to be a degraded appendage of the tourist industry, it would no longer be a commodity and would begin to embody national values. It is assumed that the artist would succeed in creating works of social significance to the degree that he was not dependent on external sources for economic survival. Evidently, the artist who addressed his work to the members of his community would not be exploiting them because he would be interacting with his audience on a personal basis, in pursuit of their common interests, rather than simply exchanging the products of his labor for personal gain. As the artist became reintegrated with his community, there would be mutual enhancement of self-respect, and a once functional economic relationship would thereby be changed into a social relationship.

Yet, without an adequate material basis, or control over their political fortunes, it would be impossible for Cubans to achieve the desired goal of existing only for themselves.[3] Thus, Guillén expresses the hope that Cubans would act to determine their own destiny:

Como un puñal, como un arpón,
el banderón americano
en tu costado de carbón.
Sucio de sangre el banderón.
Un yanqui allí, látigo en mano.

En la sombría plantación,
donde tu voz alzas en vano
y te exprimen el corazón,
sé que sofoca tu canción
un yanqui allí, látigo en mano.
. . . .

Rojo desciende de su avión
míster Smith, un cuadrumano
de la selva de Guasintón.
Hay coctel en la legación.
Un yanqui allí, látigo en mano.

Será tal vez una ilusión,
tal vez será un ensueño vano,
mas veo rodar el banderón
y arder al viento tu canción,
puesta en el mástil por tu mano.

[Like a dagger, like a harpoon,
the big American flag

in your coal-black side.
Tainted with blood the big American flag.
An American over there, whip in hand.

On the gloomy plantation,
where you raise your voice in vain
and they squeeze out your heart,
I know that he stifles your song,
An American over there, whip in hand.
. . . .

Ruddy Mr. Smith, a quadruped
from the Washington jungle,
descends from his airplane.
There are cocktails at the embassy.
An American over there, whip in hand.

Perhaps it is probably an illusion,
perhaps it is probably a vain dream,
but I see the big flag tumbling down
and your song glittering in the wind,
placed on the mast by your own hand.]

("El banderón," 2: 17-18)

But if the final goal is clearly perceived, the strategy for achieving it is not, no doubt because it was felt that struggle on the part of an unarmed Cuba to assert itself would put it in unequal combat against a more powerful United States. The recurrent image of the American armed with his whip tends to overshadow the stated desire for self-determination, and therefore attests to an underlying element of "geographical fatalism," in that proximity to the United States causes the fear of reprisal to be uppermost in the mind, and the will to political and economic reform is held in abeyance.[4]

Nevertheless, the dehumanizing structures of the plantation society, which was felt to give Cubans little opportunity for becoming the subjects of their own history, made the need for reform a recurrent theme in several of Guillén's verses. The conditions of sugar workers in particular were believed to be so intolerable that it was necessary to act to achieve social justice in their case. For that reason, the activities of the union leader, Jesús Menéndez, were considered to be of central importance to the project of liberating the Cuban working class:

Jesús trabaja y sueña. Anda por su isla, pero también sale de ella, en un gran barco de fuego. Recorre las cañas míseras, se inclina sobre su dulce angustia, habla con el cortador desollado, lo anima y lo sostiene. . . . Jesús nada dice, pero hay en sus ojos un resplandor de grávida promesa, como el de las hoces en la siega, cuando son heridas por el sol. Levanta su puño poderoso como un seguro martillo y avanza seguido de duras gargantas, que entonan en un idioma nuevo una canción ancha y alta, como un pedazo de océano. Jesús no está en el cielo, sino en la tierra; no demanda oraciones, sino lucha; no quiere sacerdotes, sino compañeros; no erige iglesias, sino sindicatos: Nadie lo podrá matar.

[Jesús works and dreams. He travels all over his island but he also leaves it in a great ship of fire. He goes through the wretched canefields, he bends over their sweet anguish, he talks to the flayed canecutter, he encourages him and supports him. . . . Jesús says nothing, but there appears in his eye a gleam of fruitful promise, like that of sickles at harvest time, when they are struck by the sun. He raises his powerful fist like a steady hammer and advances, followed by harsh throats, who intone a loud, full song in a new language, like a fragment of ocean. Jesús is not in heaven, but on earth; he does not demand prayers but struggle; he does not want priests but comrades; he does not build churches but labor unions: No one will be able to kill him.]

("Elegía a Jesús Menéndez," 1: 430, 433)

The paradoxical nature of the sugarcane—sweet to the taste and to those who own it, but a source of anguish for those who must work in the fields—gave a sense of urgency to Menéndez's task of organizing the workers into a group capable of defending its own interests. If in this instance the initiative for improving the situation of the workers is attributed to the leader rather than to the workers themselves,[5] it is because the workers are considered to be still bound to an individualistic mode of perception. Even though they are believed to be exploited as a group, Guillén refers to them in the singular in order to indicate their lack of class consciousness. The despair of the individual cane-cutter presumably derives from his perception of himself as an isolated entity who has been deprived of the enjoyment of the fruits of his labor. Once he is made to realize that his situation is identical to that of count-less others who are obliged to work for miserable wages, it is expected that his private anguish will be replaced by joyful participation in a collective movement to transform an alienated existence into one of freedom and creativity.

Despite Guillén's optimistic assessment of the irreversible changes that Menéndez's unionization of the workers introduced into the eco-nomic process, workers who are represented as "harsh throats" are not truly endowed with the subjective freedom needed to inaugurate the era of self-realization that their "loud song in a new language" seems to herald. All the activity required to create the opening onto the brighter future is undertaken by the union leader, who presumably embodies the intentions of the workers to assume mastery of their social existence. It is therefore obvious that when Menéndez dies, the sugar workers as a group are not in a position to articulate their demands in a coherent manner.[6]

That the Cuban working class of the 1940s was incapable of assuming the historical role envisaged for it by Marxists is clearly indicated by the ending of Guillén's poem. Once again, the sugar workers are not designated as revolutionary subjects; this time they depend for their freedom not on the actions of a leader within society, but on the prophetic statements enunciated by a dead leader, which would presumably create the new moment of freedom:

Venid, venid y en la alta
torre estaréis, campana y campanero;
estaremos, venid,
metal y huesos juntos que saludan
el fino, el esperado amanecer
de las raíces; el tremendo hallazgo
de una súbita estrella;
metal y huesos juntos que saludan
la paloma de vuelo popular
y verde ramo en el aire sin dueño;
el carro ya de espigas
lleno recién cortadas;
la presencia esencial
del acero y la rosa:
metal y huesos juntos que saludan
la procesión final, el ancho séquito
de la victoria.
       Entonces llegará,
General de las Cañas, con su sable
hecho de un gran relámpago bruñido;
entonces llegará,
jinete en un caballo de agua y humo,
lenta sonrisa en el saludo lento;
entonces llegará para decir,
Jesús, para decir:
—Mirad, he aquí el azúcar ya sin lágrimas.
Para decir:
—He vuelto, no temáis,
Para decir:
—Fue largo el viaje y áspero el camino.
Creció un árbol con sangre de mi herida.
Canta desde él un pájaro a la vida.
La mañana se anuncia con un trino.

[Come, come, and you will be in the
lofty belfry, bell and bell ringer;
come, and together we will be
metal and bones that greet
the fine, the awaited dawn
of the beginning; the tremendous discovery
of an unexpected star;
metal and bones that together greet

the bird of popular flight
and the green branch in the masterless air;
the cart now filled with
freshly cut ears;
the essential presence
of steel and the rose:
metal and bones that together greet
the final procession, the broad cortege
of victory.
                    Then he will come,
the General of the Canefields, with his cutlass
made from a great burnished flash of lightning;
then he will come,
the rider of a horse of water and smoke,
slow smile in the slow greeting;
then he will come to say,
Jesús, to say:
"Look, now here is sugar without tears."
To say:
"I have returned, be not afraid."
To say:
"Long was the journey and rough the road.
A tree grew with the blood from my wound.
In it a bird sings to life.
Morning is announced with a trill."]

(1: 435–36)

Like his biblical counterpart, Jesús Menéndez is now perceived to be a messianic figure, whose second coming is expected to deliver the sugar workers from the evils of the present. The insubstantial qualities with which the slain leader is endowed, and the imprecise moment when the promise of deliverance is to be fulfilled, remove the struggles of the Cuban working class from the realm of social reality. The defiant assertion made in the previous section of the poem, that Jesús Menéndez's presence could not be negated by death, now appears to have been uttered in a sociopolitical void, since the apotheosis of the union leader suspends the historical connection between Menéndez and the members of his labor union. The possibility that Menéndez will achieve a secular form of immortality through the workers' active continuation of the project of altering their relationship with other men in Cuban society is no longer taken into account. The prospect of abundance for all also becomes illusory since there is no indication of the technological changes that would transform the relationship between man and nature so that sugar and other agricultural products could be produced efficiently, making unnecessary the arduous and unrewarding labor being performed by canecutters.

With the emptying of their historical specificity, the final words attributed to Jesús Menéndez come to have a purely symbolic function, for in the meantime, Menéndez, the concrete spokesman for Cuba's sugar workers, has been transformed into the ideal champion of all the oppressed in Latin America. Situated outside time and human society, Menéndez's statements can only serve as a consolation to his implied audience, since they lack the referential force for designating the objectives to be attained by the workers of a particular country. No mention is made, for example, of how the lands owned by the United Fruit Company in Central America could be repossessed and administered for the benefit of the banana workers as a group, or of Guatemalan society as a whole.

Undoubtedly, it is the overwhelming strength of the opposition that causes the specific goals of the Cuban working class to lose their historical content.[7] If unionization in itself, with its primary focus on labor relations, was incapable of addressing the larger problem of working class subordination, its taking up the limited issue of economic rewards was often perceived as a threat to the Cuban sociopolitical system.[8] Thus, in the course of Guillén's poem, the alliance of military, financial, and political interests, both national and international, that was opposed to the labor movement tends to place the workers' struggle in parentheses. In fact, the Góngora epigraph already alludes to the ethical rather than the material strength possessed by Menéndez and the members of his union.

Nevertheless, in the broader context of Latin America, armed struggle was seen as the only means of enabling Latin Americans to assume control of their historical destiny. Contrary to the gradualist policies advocated by the Communist parties of the time,[9] Guillén proposes a violent solution to the Guatemalan situation of 1954:

> Lloraba una nube sola
> junto a la puerta del Cielo;
> yo la vi desde mi avión
> y le presté mi pañuelo.
> — ¡Guatemala,
> gemía, crespón de duelo,
> que el yanqui de nuevo tala
> bosques de sangre en tu suelo!
> Yo respondí a su desvelo:
> —Al yanqui, bala por bala,
> no más vigílale el vuelo.
>   (Pareja con el avión
>   iba el águila imperial;
>   plumas de hierro, las garras
>   abiertas para agarrar.
>   Hoy roba y roba, mañana
>   ya no te podrá robar.)

[A single cloud was weeping
near the gates of Heaven;
I saw it from my plane
and lent it my handkerchief.
"Guatemala,"
it moaned, in mourning band,
"for the American once again fells
forests of blood on your soil!"
I replied to its concern:
"As for the American, bullet for bullet,
only be on the lookout for his flight."
               (Abreast with the plane
               went the imperial eagle;
               iron feathers, talons
               open for seizing.
               Today it robs and robs, tomorrow
               it will no longer be able to rob you.)]
                       ("Balada guatemalteca," 1: 43-44)

Paradoxically, armed struggle is recommended precisely when it has proved to be ineffective, since it was the inability of Guatemala to defend itself militarily that was largely responsible for the success of the American effort to disrupt the socialist experiments of the elected government in Guatemala.[10] But if Guillén's implied audience appears incapable of reversing the political situation, the poet's expectation is evidently that his actual readers would be sufficiently convinced of the injustice done to Guatemala that they would make a concerted effort to bring about that country's freedom from American domination. In anticipation of that eventuality, the American intervention is represented as a parenthetical interlude in Guatemalan history. The parallelism and repetition that inform the poem are therefore intended to make the need for solidarity transparent to the reader.

By representing the reimposition of American control as an occasion for mourning, Guillén clearly perceives the capitalist moment in Guatemala as a period of material loss. In fact, Latin America's long existence as a colony of Europe and the United States does not permit Guillén to view the history of that continent as a progressive march from an era of scarcity for the many to an era of abundance for all.[11] For the poet, American exploitation of Guatemala's essential resources does not constitute an improvement on the deficiencies of the past; rather it constitutes the arresting of an earlier moment of self-sufficiency. In view of what is perceived to be a distortion of the legitimate course of Guatemalan history, violence is advocated as a means of negating an unproductive present so as to enable a period of prosperity to come into existence.

Guillén's insistence that nationalization is indispensable for socio-economic well-being stems from the well-known fact that the structures of dependent capitalism do not afford Latin Americans the advantages that capitalism offers to residents of the metropolis. While capitalism is generally held responisble for man's alienation from nature, from his fellow human beings, and from himself, it is usually admitted that the seeds of the socialist future are embedded in the capitalist present. Even though the social relationships of class society tend to be deplored because of their competitiveness and their basis in a structure of in-equality, the increase in productivity made possible by the techno-logical inventions of capitalism is generally held to be historically necessary for supplying the material needs of men in the classless society.[12] To Guillén, however, the capitalist phase had to be super-seded, not because the productive forces in Latin America were suffi-ciently developed to make the transition to socialism virtually inevitable, but because capitalism in Latin America meant the existence of class distinctions, without the accompanying increase in the standard of living of the general population.

In one instance, the desire is expressed for existing social divisions to be modified:

> Virgen de la Caridad,
> que desde un peñón de cobre
> esperanza das al pobre
> y al rico seguridad.
> En tu criolla bondad,
> ¡oh madre!, siempre creí,
> por eso pido de ti
> que si esa bondad me alcanza
> des al rico la esperanza,
> la seguridad a mí.

> [Virgin of Charity
> who, from a copper rock,
> gives hope to the poor
> and security to the rich.
> In your creole goodness,
> oh mother!, I always believed.
> Therefore I beg you,
> that if that goodness extends to me,
> give the hope to the rich,
> the security to me.]

("A la Virgen de la Caridad," 2: 180)

If the ironic appeal to Cuba's patron saint appears to be grounded on a view of the social order as sanctioned by divine right, it also points to the atemporal postulates from which a human arrangement derives its legitimacy. Yet, what seems natural by virtue of religious sanction often relies on the use of force to hold it in place.

As was mentioned in previous chapters, the military tended to play a fundamental role in the maintenance of internal social divisions. In Cuba, for example, the soldier's primary task was to contain the demands of the working class for improved living conditions. However, Guillén perceives this situation as characteristic of Latin America as a whole:

Te faltó quien viniera,
soldado, y al oído te dijera:
"Eres esclavo, esclavo
como esos bueyes gordos,
ciegos, tranquilos, sordos,
que pastan bajo el sol meneando el rabo.
Esta paz es culpable.
¡Cuándo será que hable
tu boca, y que tu rudo pecho grite,
se rebele y agite!
Tú, paria en Cuba, solo y miserable,
puedes rugir con voz del Continente:
la sangre que te lleva en su corriente
es la misma en Bolivia, en Guatemala,
en Brasil, en Haití. . . Tierras oscuras,
tierras de alambre para vuelo y ala,
quemadas por iguales calenturas,
secas a golpes de puñal y bala,
y en las que garras duras
están con pico y pala
día y noche cavando sepulturas.
Y tú cuerpidesnudo
mohoso, pétreo, mudo,
ofreciendo tu cuello,
tus uñas, tu resuello,
para encender sortijas,
empujar automóviles,
y sucio ver el vientre de tus hijas,
con las manos inmóviles."

[You needed someone to come,
soldier, and whisper to you:
"You are a slave, a slave
like those fat, blind,
calm, deaf oxen,
which graze in the sun, wagging their tails.
This peace is to blame.
When will your mouth
speak, and your rough breast shout,
rebel, and stir!

You, a pariah in Cuba, alone and miserable,
can roar with the voice of the Continent:
the blood which carries you in its tide
is the same in Bolivia, in Guatemala,
in Brazil, in Haiti . . . Dark lands,
lands of wire for flight and wings,
burnt by the same fevers,
arid from dagger thrusts and bullets,
and where tough claws
are digging graves day and night
with pick and shovel.
And you, naked body,
musty, stony, dumb,
offering your neck,
your nails, your breath,
to make rings glitter,
push cars,
and see the womb of your daughters sullied,
with motionless hands."]

("Elegía a un soldado vivo," 1: 190-191)

Guillén's reference to the soldier in essentialist terms is intended to indicate the surrender of humanity entailed in being a servant of international capital. Not only is the soldier said to be risking his life for a small material reward, but in performing a task that merely facilitates the enrichment of others, he is considered to be alienated from himself and from the members of his society. At the same time, the soldier seems to be unaware of his self-betrayal, since he comes to perceive himself solely in terms of his instrumental role. Yet the loss of subjectivity is apparently not irreversible. Because the poem is rhetorically addressed to the soldier, the poet's intention is evidently to heighten the implied listener's awareness of his lack of personal freedom. By presenting the soldier with a vision of himself as a disembodied object, Guillén clearly expects him to refuse his secondary condition and to choose to become a free person.

Essential to Guillén's project of creating a political consciousness in his implied audience is the linkage of the military situation in Cuba with that of other Latin American republics so as to make transparent the soldier's participation in a widespread system of injustice. Presumably, once the soldier is made to realize that his hostility is directed against his own people, he will cease to act against the interests of his fellow citizens and choose to be restored to a plane of equality with them. Consequently, the poet attempts to facilitate this process by addressing the soldier as the peasant that he was rather than as the professional that he has become:

¿Será posible que tu mano agraria,
la que empujó el arado
sobre la tierra paria;
tu mano campesina, hoy de soldado,
que no robó al ganado
la sombra de su selva solitaria,
ora quitarme quiera
mi pan de cada día,
para hacer aún más gorda la chequera
del amo fiero que en tu máuser fía?
¡Di que no, di que no! Di, compañero,
que tu hermano es primero:
que vienes de la tierra, eres de tierra
y a la tierra darás tu amor postrero;
que no irás a la guerra
a morir por petróleo o por asfalto,
mientras tu impar caldero
de primordial maíz bosteza falto;

[Can it be possible that your agrarian hand
which pushed the plough
on your pariah land,
your peasant hand, today a soldier's,
which did not rob from the cattle
the shade of their solitary pasture,
now wishes to take away
my daily bread,
in order to make still fatter the checkbook
of the proud master who trusts in your Mauser?
Say no, say no! Say, comrade,
that your brother comes first:
that you come from the land, that you belong to the land
and that you will give your utmost love to the land;
that you will not go to war
to die for petroleum or for asphalt,
while your only pot
gapes empty of primordial maize;]

(1: 191-92)

By referring the soldier back to his class origins, Guillén evidently
believes in the existence of an authentic self that remains unaffected
by the subsequent existential choices made by the subject. The soldier's
essential self is thus assumed to lie buried beneath his actual appearance as a servant of international capital. The soldier's internalization
of the expectations of others is therefore regarded as a temporary
aberration that will be reversed by an appropriate process of enlightenment. That the soldier may have chosen to become an oppressor of
his people is thereby excluded from consideration, since it is assumed

that the soldier's desire to control his peers is simply an expression of false consciousness.

The belief in the existence of an original self means that the soldier cannot seek to be reconciled with himself and with his peers from the place that he actually occupies in the social hierarchy. Inasmuch as it is assumed that he lacks the fulfillment that he once enjoyed as a peasant, his quest for rehumanization is expected to begin with the renunciation of his current mode of existence and to culminate in his return to the realm of nature:

> ¡Ya no volveré al cuartel,
> suelto por calles y plazas,
> yo mismo, Pedro Cortés!
>
> Yo mismo dueño de mí,
> ya por fin libre de guardias,
> de uniforme y de fusil.
>
> Podré a mi pueblo correr,
> y gritar, cuando me vean:
> ¡aquí está Pedro Cortés!
>
> Podré trabajar al sol,
> y en la tierra que me espera,
> con mi arado labrador.
>
> Ser hombre otra vez de paz,
> cargar niños, besar frentes,
> cantar, reír y saltar.
>
> [I will no longer return to the barracks,
> free in the streets and squares,
> I myself, Pedro Cortés!
>
> The selfsame I, master of myself,
> now finally free from guard duties,
> from a uniform and from a rifle.
>
> I will be able to run to my people,
> and to shout, when they see me:
> "Here is Pedro Cortés!"
>
> I will be able to work in the sun,
> and on the land that awaits me,
> with my farmer's plough.
>
> To be a man of peace once again,
> to carry children, kiss foreheads,
> sing, laugh and leap.]

("Soldado libre," 1: 196)

Here the "free" individual comes to be perceived as a preexistent man rather than as a "new man," who, upon contact with nature, spontaneously recovers his expressiveness and the ability to engage in uninhibited relations with others whom he now regards as equals. Thus, the actual guardian of the status quo is seen as the agent of a more just society once he has discarded the symbols that serve to estrange him from the members of his community. By exchanging his instruments of violence for productive tools, the soldier is viewed as no longer standing in a relationship of dominance or submission to other men. Instead, he is perceived as having exchanged his one-dimensional existence for a more fulfilling round of activities marked by versatility. The persona's resumption of the peasant's life is also expected to end his economic alienation since he would no longer be a servant of an impersonal system. Having recovered his self-possession, he would now be transforming nature to suit his own purposes. However, the land would not be possessed as a commodity, since it is believed to exist primarily to serve the persona's need to engage in creative labor. As a result, the separation between man and nature, labor and capital, would be overcome.

The authenticity that is considered to be innate in the peasant explains his presumed centrality to the revolutionary project. Unlike the soldier, the peasant was not fully integrated into the capitalist economy and therefore could be regarded as more genuinely Cuban.[13] Since the industrial proletariat in Cuba was not only a numerically small, but also a relatively privileged group that owed its existence to those sectors of the economy that were most dominated by international capital,[14] the peasant, by virtue of his marginality in that economy, could be regarded as the most exploited member of the society, and as such could replace the traditional Marxist group as the ideal revolutionary subject.[15]

By the same token, the city is rejected as the locus of revolutionary activity, undoubtedly because of the wider acceptance on the part of its residents of the competitive norms of the metropolis. In an anticipation of what would become a fundamental tenet of Guevaran Marxism in Guillén's poem, the countryside is depicted as the more humanizing environment, facilitating the transformation of the previously alienated persona into a fully socialized individual.[16]

The hypothetical conversion of soldier to civilian presumably embodies the general will of the military to transfer their loyalty to the community at large. However, the fact that Pedro Cortés's intentions are cast in the tense of probability indicates the poet's awareness that mutually enhancing relationships between self and others are not that easily achieved. The difference in power between soldier and people as well as the hierarchical structure of the army were unlikely to result in such an unproblematic instance of social integration. Moreover, Pedro Cortés's need to discard the trappings of his office before being fully accepted into the community indicates the extent to which relations between civilian and soldier were constrained by the latter's social role. As a result, the following verses represent an additional attempt on the part of the poet to create an awareness of mutuality between civilian and soldier:

No sé por qué piensas tú,
soldado, que te odio yo,
si somos la misma cosa
yo,
tú.

Tú eres pobre, lo soy yo;
soy de abajo, lo eres tú;
¿de dónde has sacado tú,
soldado, que te odio yo?

Me duele que a veces tú
te olvides de quién soy yo;
caramba, si yo soy tú,
lo mismo que tú eres yo.

Pero no por eso yo
he de malquererte, tú;
si somos la misma cosa,
yo,
tú,
no sé por qué piensas tú,
soldado, que te odio yo.

Ya nos veremos yo y tú,
juntos en la misma calle,
hombro con hombro, tú y yo,
sin odios ni yo ni tú,
pero sabiendo tú y yo,
a dónde vamos yo y tú . . .
¡No sé por qué piensas tú,
soldado, que te odio yo!

[I don't know why you think,
soldier, that I hate you;
why, we are the same thing,
I,
you.

You are poor, so am I;
I am from below, so are you;
where have you gotten the idea,
soldier, that I hate you?

It hurts me that at times you
forget who I am;
gee, why, I am you,
just as you are I.

But not for that reason I
have to dislike you;
why, we are the same thing,
I,
you,
I don't know why you think,
soldier, that I hate you.

Now we will see each other, I and you,
together in the same street,
shoulder to shoulder, you and I,
without hatred, neither I nor you,
but knowing you and I,
where we are going, I and you . . .
I don't know why you think,
soldier, that I hate you!]

("No sé por qué piensas tú . . .," 1: 175-76)

The formulation of the speaker's statements in the familiar mode of
address demonstrates the wish to erase the social distance that separates
the speaker from his ostensible listener. The soldier is therefore perceived not as the repressive authority figure that he is, but as the comrade in arms that the persona would like him to be. The shifting of the
personal pronouns is intended by the speaker to convince his hypothetical listener of their interchangeability, and as a result, to persuade him
of their common identity. Since most soldiers in pre-Revolutionary
Cuba were of proletarian origin,[17] the speaker's assumption is that the
soldier would be guided to act by his class origins rather than by his
professionalism. In that case, the soldier would become aware of his
fundamental brotherhood with the Cuban people, and would cease to
engage in acts of violence against them, since that would be akin to
engaging in violence against the self. However, the rhetorical return to
the original condition of apartness suggests a recognition by the poet of
the difficulty of achieving more than a grammatical sense of reciprocity
between the collective self and the members of an all-powerful army.
Unlike the actual gap that is perceived to exist between speaker and soldier, the aspiration to solidarity is deferred to a future moment, whose
possibilities of being fulfilled are disrupted when the syntactical link between both subjects is severed by the final separation of the "you" and
the "I."

Guillén's recognition of the unlikelihood of persuading the members
of a professional army to cease acting as such and to join forces with the

members of their former social class leads to a search for other forms of
alliances. In the attempt to create a revolutionary will, the desire is
expressed for racial antagonisms to be overcome:

> Para hacer esta muralla,
> tráiganme todas las manos:
> los negros, sus manos negras,
> los blancos, sus blancas manos.
> Ay,
> una muralla que vaya
> desde la playa hasta el monte,
> desde el monte hasta la playa, bien,
> allá sobre el horizonte.
> . . . .
> Al corazón del amigo,
> abre la muralla;
> al veneno y al puñal,
> cierra la muralla;
> al mirto y la yerbabuena,
> abre la muralla;
> al diente de la serpiente,
> cierra la muralla;
> al ruiseñor en la flor,
> abre la muralla . . .
>
> [To build this wall,
> bring me all hands:
> blacks, their black hands,
> whites, their white hands.
> Oh,
> a wall that extends
> from the beach to the mountains,
> from the mountains to the beach, indeed,
> way beyond the horizon.
> . . . .
> To the heart of the friend,
> open the wall;
> to poison and the dagger,
> close the wall;
> to the myrtle and the mint,
> open the wall;
> to the serpent's tooth,
> close the wall;
> to the nightingale on the flower,
> open the wall . . .]

("La muralla," 2: 14-17)

Hands ordinarily separated are expected to be linked in the common
project of national defense. Since it was felt that the regular army could

not be persuaded to adopt a stance of revolutionary nationalism, it was hoped that the ordinary citizens of Cuba would give priority to the pursuit of social harmony, for the absence of conflict was clearly perceived as the highest good. Thus, closure to alien forces was seen as necessary for bringing a harmonious state into being.

The call for an end to divisiveness within the society evidently stemmed from Guillén's view that injustice in Cuba was less the result of stratification within the society than from the political and economic limitations imposed by external forces. Consequently, it is assumed that the forging of alliances across racial and class lines would bring an end to the marginality of many Cuban citizens and result in a period of internal development.[18]

While cooperative relationships were perceived to be necessary for negating the divisive influence of alien forces, it was not always believed that the deficiencies of the present could be remedied by an evolutionary strategy. Impatience with the stagnation of the existing socioeconomic system leads to a desire for its violent overthrow:

Onda negribermeja
de obreros de agria ceja
y niños con la cara vieja,
heridos por el ojo fijo del policía.
Tierra donde la sangre ensucia el día
y hay pies en detenida velocidad de salto
y gargantas de queja y no de grito
y gargantas de grito y no de queja
y voces de cañaverales en alto
y lo que se dice y no está escrito
. . . .

Casa de vecindad, patio del Mar Caribe,
con mi guitarra de áspero son,
aquí estoy, para ver si me saco del pecho
una canción.
Una canción de sueño desatado,
una simple canción de muerte y vida
con que saludar el futuro ensangrentado,
rojo como las sábanas, como los muslos, como el lecho
de una mujer recién parida.

[Blackish red wave
of workers with bitter brows
and children with old faces,
wounded by the policeman's steady eye.
Land where blood soils the day
and there are feet in the parked gear of a leap
and throats of complaint but not of screams
and throats of screams but not of complaint

and raised voices of canefields
and what is said and is not written
. . . .

Tenement house, patio of the Caribbean Sea,
with my harsh-sounding guitar,
here I am, to see if I can express from my heart
a song.
A song of an unfettered dream,
a simple song of life and death
with which to greet the bloody future,
red like the sheets, like the thighs, like the bed
of a woman who has just given birth.]

("Casa de vecindad," 2: 19)

Whereas many of the poet's earlier verses had been oriented toward a gradualist process of change, the hopelessness of the situation described here appears to make violent upheaval inevitable. Given the poet's organic view of society, it was felt that a new era of creativity could be ushered in only by a fundamental alteration of the social structure.

Perhaps it was his awareness of the outcome of the Chinese struggle for liberation that caused Guillén to become convinced of the efficacy of direct action. For in China, the revolutionary process was believed to have brought a more just society into being:

Ay, cuando Wang Tse-Yu nació,
lunas, amargas lunas antes,
antes
de la gran revolución,
cayó como un pedrusco negro,
pasó como un pequeño perro,
lloró sin cuna y sin pañuelo,
antes, muchas lunas antes,
antes
de la gran revolución.

Hoy he visto a Wang Tse-Yu:
¿Querrás decirme, amigo,
qué estabas haciendo tú,
alto el corazón en punta,
los negros ojos llenos de luz
y tu gran país labrado
en dura llama y cielo azul?
. . . .

Gané mi tierra con mi lanza
(me respondió Wang Tse-Yu).
Gané mi lanza con mi vida,
gané mi vida con mi sangre,
gané mi sangre con mi sueño . . .

Hoy mi sueño es estar despierto
(me respondió Wang Tse-Yu).

[Alas, when Wang Tse-Yu was born,
moons, bitter moons before,
before
the great revolution,
he fell like a dark boulder,
he arrived like a little dog,
he cried without a cradle and without a handkerchief,
before, many moons before,
before
the great revolution.

Today I saw Wang Tse-Yu:
Do you want to tell me, friend,
what you were doing,
your heart beating proud,
your black eyes filled with light
and your great country built
in a harsh flame and blue sky?
. . . .

I won my land with my lance
(Wang Tse-Yu replied to me).
I won my lance with my life,
I won my life with my blood,
I won my blood with my dream . . .
Today my dream is to be awake
(Wang Tse-Yu replied to me).]

("Tres canciones chinas," 2: 30-31)

To the average Chinese citizen, the coming of the revolution evidently meant an end to material deprivation. However, even more significant was the personal transformation that was supposed to ensue from participation in a project of social reconstruction. When man becomes a conscious historical actor instead of being at the mercy of circumstances as under the previous social system, he presumably ceases to be a stranger to himself and begins to recognize himself in the products of his labor.[19] Having assumed responsibility for the ongoing transformation of his objective situation, he apparently begins to experience himself as the center of his world—an attitude said to be reflected in his personal appearance. The revolutionary's altered perceptions of his place in the world are also taken to be a sign of his humanization as he acquires a socialized consciousness and comes to identify his own well-being with that of his community.[20]

However, the socialist ideal of the merger of the individual and the collective domains was not espoused by all members of Chinese society.

To some individuals, the passing of the capitalist system was a matter for regret:

> ¡Oh volver nuevamente, volver,
> dueño huraño, a mis siembras de arroz!
> —¿A tus siembras de arroz?
> Es inútil volver:
> Sembró en ellas el pueblo su voz.
>
> Entre lotos marchitos bogar
> y añorar su pasado esplendor . . .
> —¿Su pasado esplendor?
> Es inútil bogar:
> Mira el loto: decora un tractor.
>
> [Oh, to return once more, to return,
> shy owner, to my rice fields!
> "To your rice fields?
> It is useless to return:
> The people sowed their voice in them."
>
> To row among wilted lotus
> and to yearn for their past splendor . . .
> "Their past splendor?
> It is useless to row:
> Look at the lotus: it decorates a tractor."]
>
> (2: 29)

Even as the former landowner laments the loss of his private property, the representatives of the new order perceive the idea of communally owned fields as a means of ensuring abundance for the many rather than for the few. Yet, while the property relations of capitalism are rejected, its technological inventions are not because they are considered essential for improving the productivity of the land and are therefore necessary to the socialist project of freeing man from the constraints of necessity and installing him in the realm of freedom.[21] Given the "new man's" recognition of himself as primarily a social being, the aim of this increased productivity is evidently not to benefit the individual but to satisfy the needs of all members of the community.

The dialogic situation in the poem makes it clear that Guillén is in favor of the socialization of private property, for the nostalgic yearnings of the landowner are revealed to be not only egoistic but effete. Therefore, the basic idea that informs the poem is that concern for the needs of the majority should supersede the possession of property as a commodity—an idea that is restated in the following verses:

> —El alquiler se cumplió:
> te tienes que mudar;

ay, pero el problema es serio,
muy serio,
pero el problema es muy serio,
porque no hay con qué pagar.
. . . .

—Escuche, amigo casero,
ayer me citó el Juzgado,
y dije que no he pagado
porque no tengo dinero,
y estoy parado.
Yo no me voy a la calle,
porque la lluvia me moja;
. . . .

Conozco hoteles vacíos
y casas sin habitantes:
¿cómo voy a estar de pie,
con tantos puestos vacantes?

["The rent is due:
you have to move;
ah, but the problem is serious,
very serious,
but the problem is very serious,
because there is no means of paying."
. . . .

"Listen, Mr. Landlord,
yesterday the Court summoned me,
and I said that I did not pay
because I have no money,
and I am out of work.
I am not going out on the street,
because the rain will wet me;
. . . .

I know empty hotels
and houses without occupants:
how can I be on my feet,
with so many empty places?"]

("Son del desahucio," 1: 204-6)

Unlike the Chinese landowner, whose ownership of private property was
a fond memory, the Cuban landlord of the 1930s had his right to ownership upheld by the prevailing laws. Nevertheless, despite the judgment
of the courts, the evicted tenant has an alternative view of social justice,
since he perceives housing as a basic right to be guaranteed to all citizens
rather than as an item to be regulated by the marketplace.

    That the persona is made to pose this concept as a rhetorical
question rather than as an assertion indicates that the objective conditions

were not yet ripe for the socialist experiment to be put into practice in Cuba. More than twenty years elapsed between the writing of Guillén's poem and the attempt of Fidel Castro's government to solve the problems of unemployment and homelessness faced by Guillén's persona. However, even though the alternative view of the relationship between self and society is articulated in the language of virtuality, once the Cuban Revolution became a historical reality it became possible to regard the verses cited above as a prophetic indicator of revolutionary change.

CHAPTER 6

THE
REVOLUTIONARY
ALTERNATIVE

That the Cuban Revolution did
not seek merely to transform the material conditions of man is well
known. Ernesto (Che) Guevara's pronouncements on the need to
create a "new man,"[1] as well as the debate regarding moral and material incentives in economic policy,[2] are a clear indication that the
revolutionary leadership not only undertook to restructure the socioeconomic institutions of Cuban society, but also aimed at effecting
a complete "transformation of political culture."[3] Writers and intellectuals were expected to contribute to this project by endorsing revolutionary values in their work.[4] Aware that a socialist consciousness
could not be readily induced in a people long exposed to bourgeois
modes of thought, the revolutionary government created a number
of cultural organs—publishing houses, journals, literary prizes, and
conferences—to provide writers with a forum for mediating between
the repudiated points of reference and the desired moral order. To
writers who feared that support by and for the Revolution automatically
delimited their sphere of activity, Fidel Castro's dictum, "Within the
Revolution, everything; against the Revolution, no rights at all,"[5]
a position that was subsequently legitimized in the Constitution,[6] was
intended as a guarantee that official policy was not synonymous
with restraints on artistic expression.

In Guillén's case, the expectation that his poetry would reflect
a revolutionary posture was not perceived as a curtailment of his
artistic freedom, since, as we saw in chapter 5, Guillén had long advocated the socialist measures now being called into existence by the
regime. It is therefore not surprising that he would choose to com-
memorate selected moments in recent Cuban history, such as the

literacy campaign and the implementation of the programs for agrarian reform. But it is the poem, "Tengo" (I have), that best summarizes his attitude toward the realization of the object of his desire:

> Cuando me veo y toco
> yo, Juan sin Nada no más ayer,
> y hoy Juan con Todo,
> y hoy con todo,
> vuelvo los ojos, miro,
> me veo y toco
> y me pregunto cómo ha podido ser.

> [When I see and touch myself,
> I, John with Nothing only yesterday,
> and today John with Everything,
> and today with everything,
> I turn my eyes, I look,
> I see and touch myself
> and I wonder how it could have been.]

("Tengo," 2: 78)

Here the persona reflects upon his instant transition from a state of destitution to one of proud ownership. However, for the speaking subject, ownership is less defined by an accumulation of tangible objects than by a radical change in self-perception, which results in an altered relationship between self and world. Indeed, the basis of self-interest is so fundamentally restated as to have established an equivalence between personal fortune and the national patrimony:

> Tengo, vamos a ver,
> tengo el gusto de andar por mi país,
> dueño de cuanto hay en él,
> mirando bien de cerca lo que antes
> no tuve ni podía tener.
> Zafra puedo decir,
> monte puedo decir,
> ciudad puedo decir,
> ejército decir,
> ya míos para siempre y tuyos, nuestros,

> [I have, let's see,
> I have the pleasure of walking around my country,
> master of all there is in it,
> looking very closely at what
> I did not and could not have before.
> Sugar crop, I can say,
> mountain, I can say,
> city, I can say,
> army say,

now mine forever and yours, ours,]

(2: 78–79)

Since the boundaries between self and other have become blurred,
the satisfaction of basic individual needs is held in abeyance and appears
almost as an afterthought in this catalog of recently acquired rights:

Tengo, vamos a ver,
que ya aprendí a leer,
a contar,
tengo que ya aprendí a escribir
y a pensar
y a reír.
Tengo que ya tengo
donde trabajar
y ganar
lo que me tengo que comer.
Tengo, vamos a ver,
tengo lo que tenía que tener.

[I have, let's see,
like I already learned to read,
to count,
I have, like I already learned to write
and to think
and to laugh.
I have, like I now have
a place to work
and earn
what I need to eat.
I have, let's see,
I have what I had to have.]

(2: 80)

Even these objects of appropriation are not expressive of singularity,
for if they signify the acquisition of properties hitherto unimaginable
to the enunciating-I, they also point to a condition that he shares
with an entire social class. The voice of the speaking subject therefore presents itself as a communal one, celebrating the end of necessity
and announcing the possibility of harmonious relations in an ideal
community, in which all obvious social differences are erased:

Tengo, vamos a ver,
tengo el gusto de ir
yo, campesino, obrero, gente simple,
tengo el gusto de ir
(es un ejemplo)
a un banco y hablar con el administrador,

no en inglés,
no en señor,
sino decirle compañero como se dice en español.

Tengo, vamos a ver,
que siendo un negro
nadie me puede detener
a la puerta de un dancing o de un bar.
O bien en la carpeta de un hotel
gritarme que no hay pieza,
una mínima pieza y no una pieza colosal,
una pequeña pieza donde yo pueda descansar.

[I have, let's see,
I have the pleasure of going,
I, a peasant, a worker, an ordinary person,
I have the pleasure of going
(it's an example)
to a bank and speaking to the manager,
not in English,
not in Sir,
but calling him brother as one says in Spanish.

I have, let's see,
like being black
no one can stop me
at the door of a dance hall or a bar.
Or else in the lobby of a hotel
shout at me that there is no room,
a tiny room and not a great big room,
a small room where I can rest.]

(2: 79)

It is interesting to note that the persona has taken no active part in bringing this state of affairs into being. In fact, in confessing his astonishment at "how it could have been," he demonstrates the aptness of one definition of the Cuban situation as an instance of "revolutionary paternalism."[7] Despite the note of inevitability on which the poem ends ("I have what I had to have"), the process of change to which it refers is anterior to the "when" of the opening lines, and consequently one is led to assume that it was the fulfillment of the character's needs that sparked his recognition that there had been a series of lacks in his life.

Be that as it may, the acquisition of certain elemental rights by the formerly dispossessed now causes the present to appear as a unique moment of plenitude. Marginality is believed to be transcended when one has access to all areas of the national territory and is able to apply the possessive adjective to its institutions. The political events that made this possible therefore come to be regarded as a privileged moment of origin for both man and society, since they are thought to have created a higher form of existence out of the nothingness and deprivations of yesterday.

The nature of the new departure is indicated by "Puedes?" (Can You?), where the virtues of a non-mercenary mode of interaction are affirmed. Through the dialogic structure of the poem, a neo-pastoral vision is expressed, in which the natural elements are shown to exist in and for themselves, as companions to man, rather than as resources to be exploited by him for profit:

> ¿Puedes venderme el aire que pasa entre tus dedos
> y te golpea la cara y te despeina?
> ¿Tal vez podrías venderme cinco pesos de viento,
> o más, quizás venderme una tormenta?
> ¿Acaso el aire fino
> me venderías, el aire
> (no todo) que recorre
> en tu jardín corolas y corolas,
> en tu jardín para los pájaros,
> diez pesos de aire fino?
>
>> El aire gira y pasa
>> en una mariposa.
>> Nadie lo tiene, nadie.
>
> [Can you sell me the air that passes through your fingers
> and strikes your face and messes up your hair?
> Could you perhaps sell me five pesos' worth of wind,
> or better, maybe sell me a storm?
> Perhaps you could sell me
> some clean air, the air
> (not all of it) which runs through
> corollas and corollas in your garden,
> in your garden for the birds,
> ten pesos' worth of clean air?
>
>> The air turns and passes
>> on a butterfly.
>> Nobody owns it, nobody.]

("¿Puedes?," 2: 104–5)

But the poem focuses on items of differential value; the air and the sky, which serve as the organizing principle for the first two stanzas, are not ordinarily salable commodities, as are water and land, around which the two final verses are ordered. However, the recurrence of key phrases, as in the refrain, "Nobody owns it (them), nobody," and the parallelism that informs the poem, are strategies that attempt to negate the opposition between both sets of elements and render them indistinguishable to the reader. Thus, the concept of private property is emptied of meaning, and money is revealed to be irrelevant and contingent, as the continuity between man and nature is restored, without the mediation of the market-place.[8]

In this context, it is assumed that once the connection between price and value is severed, pleasurability returns to natural phenomena, which once again recover their autonomy. With the transitivity accorded by the poem to the natural world, property ceases to be an object of social division that pits man in a competitive struggle against his neighbor for monopolistic control of it. If anything, use of the land rather than its value as a term in a commercial system of exchange is stressed:

> La tierra tuya es mía.
> Todos los pies la pisan.
> Nadie la tiene, nadie.

> [Your land is mine.
> All feet tread it.
> Nobody owns it, nobody.]

(2: 106)

An egalitarian social order is thereby posited as the highest good whereby the general well-being of all assumes primacy over individual economic success.

The underlying assumption of such a vision is a belief in the brotherhood of man. Thus, concern is expressed for people in other parts of the globe, where existential conditions militate against the achievement of a similar community of interests among men:

> Ésta es el hambre. Un animal
> todo colmillo y ojo.
> No se harta en una mesa.
> Nadie lo engaña ni distrae.
> No se contenta
> con un almuerzo o una cena.
> Anuncia siempre sangre.
> Ruge como león, aprieta como boa,
> piensa como persona.

> El ejemplar que aquí se ofrece
> fue cazado en la India (suburbios de Bombay),
> pero existe en estado más o menos salvaje
> en otras muchas partes.

> No acercarse.

> [This is hunger. An animal
> all fangs and eyes.
> It does not get its fill at a table.

Nobody diverts it nor wards it off.
It is not content
with a lunch or a supper.
It always announces blood.
It roars like a lion, squeezes like a boa,
thinks like a person.

The specimen displayed here
was caught in India (slums of Bombay),
but it exists in a more or less wild state
in many other places.

Keep away.]

("El hambre," 2: 232)

Through the metaphorical language of the poem, a graphic image of the dire consequences of human neglect is created. And, in a paraphrase of René Depestre, one could say that the implication here is that phenomena like hunger, which are brutal forces that undermine social harmony, have been controlled in Cuba through the efforts of the revolutionary government.[9]

It is this perception of Cuba as a nation where problems that alienate man from his neighbor have been resolved that explains Cuba's presumed centrality to the struggle for social justice in the rest of the hemisphere. That Cuba has succeeded in altering the conditions of existence of its own population is not considered sufficient cause for celebration. The exemplary nature of the Cuban experience is believed to require recognition by the significant others in Latin America before the revolutionary gesture will have meaning.[10] A familiar chronicle of ills— weak economies geared to the export of a single product in a fluctuating world market, rudimentary institutions unresponsive to the needs of the general population, a disenfranchised majority, social cleavages— facilitates the articulation of an alternative system of relationships. Cuba's recent experience seems to stand as a viable model for other Latin Americans to follow in acting on their world. But even as language aspires to maintain the illusion of a common cause with the sister republics of Latin America, once the attempt is made to ground the lessons of Cuba in the larger hemispheric context, conditions begin to lose their specificity and the likelihood of creating a new historical situation in Latin America becomes indeterminate. Thus, in "Brasil— Copacabana," the anticipated revolutionary moment loses its immediacy and remains suspended in a future eternally on the horizon:

Lo vi, en La Habana.
Lo vi, no lo soñé.

Palacios de antiguo mármol
para el que vivió sin zapatos.
Castillos donde el obrero reposa
sentado a la diestra de su obra.
El cigarral de la duquesa
para la hija de Juan, que está enferma.
La montaña y la playa y el vichy y el caviar
para los que antes no tenían donde estar.

¿Y aquí en Copacabana, aquí?
También lo vi.
Pues aunque todavía
es un sueño,
siento venir el día,
ha de llegar el día,
se oye rugir el día
con el viente nordeste de Pernambuco y de Bahía,
un día de sangre y pólvora bajo el sol brasileño.

[I saw it in Havana.
I saw it, it was no dream.

Palaces of ancient marble
for he who wore no shoes.
Castles where the worker rests
seated on the right side of his labor.
The orchard of the duchess
for John's daughter, who is ill.
The mountain and the beach and the vichy and the caviar
for those who had no place to stay before.

And here in Copacabana, here?
I saw it too.
Well even though
it is still a dream,
I feel the day coming,
the day must come,
one hears the day roaring
with the northeast wind from Pernambuco and Bahia,
a day of blood and gunpowder under the Brazilian sun.]
                              ("Brasil—Copacabana," 2: 113-14)

What is now a political reality in Havana is perceived as a utopian dream in Copacabana, and the chances of that dream being realized recede with each progressively more emphatic attempt to announce its imminence. The apocalyptic vision of the process of social change in Brazil simply emphasizes its removal to a dimension beyond human time.

No doubt the difficulty of envisaging the revolutionary future of Latin America in more concrete terms lies in the very fact that the future has yet to occur, and so, by definition, is not readily transposed into familiar categories.[11] At the same time, while it is evident that the Revolution represents a moment of rupture in Cuban history, an effort is made to restore continuity by embedding the actions of the revolutionary vanguard in a previous moment of national liberation:

> Garra de los garroteros,
> uñas de yanquis ladrones
> de ingenios azucareros:
> ¡a devolver los millones,
> que son para los obreros!
> La nube en rayo bajó,
> ay, Cuba, que yo lo vi;
> el águila se espantó,
> yo lo vi;
> la coyunda se rompió,
> yo lo vi;
> el pueblo canta, cantó,
> cantando está el pueblo así:
> —Vino Fidel y cumplió
> lo que prometió Martí.
>
> [Clutch of the loan sharks,
> nails of the Yankee robbers
> of sugar factories:
> to return the millions
> that go to the workers!
> The cloud descended in a lightning flash,
> oh, Cuba, for I saw it;
> the eagle got scared,
> I saw it;
> the yoke snapped,
> I saw it;
> the people sing, sang,
> the people are singing this:
> "Fidel came and fulfilled
> that which Martí promised."]

("Se acabó," 2: 166)

In view of Castro's redistributive policies, the appeal to Martí evidently goes beyond the ritual invocation of Martí's name by earlier leftist politicians,[12] and therefore serves to legitimize the perception of the present as the fulfillment of an earlier prophecy.

Despite such attempts at minimizing the strangeness of recent events, there are some individuals to whom the disjuncture is all too apparent. Theirs is not the euphoria of the crowd, for they regard the new social arrangements as a threat to their personal well-being. For them, exile is preferable to continued existence under a regime from which they feel increasingly estranged. Although their departure is viewed by the revolutionary leadership as a blessing, in that it facilitates the process of political consolidation,[13] to Guillén their emigration signifies their displacement to a metaphysical void, since it involves a decentering of culture without the possibility of creating a new system of reference. In Guillén's view, arrival in the United States represents a series of negations for Cubans, not the least of which is the inability to articulate their own sense of being:

> Tú, que partiste de Cuba,
> responde tú,
> ¿dónde hallarás verde y verde,
> azul y azul,
> palma y palma bajo el cielo?
> Responde tú.
>
> Tú, que tu lengua olvidaste,
> responde tú,
> y en lengua extraña masticas
> el güel y el yu,
> ¿cómo vivir puedes mudo?
> Responde tú.
>
> [You, who left Cuba,
> answer me,
> where will you find green and green,
> blue and blue,
> palm and palm under the sky?
> Answer me.
>
> You, who forgot your language,
> answer me,
> and in a strange tongue mumble
> (g)well and jou,
> how can you live in silence?
> Answer me.]

("Responde tú . . .," 2: 122-23)

The Spanish of the exile is not regarded as a valid means of self-expression; it is seen, rather, as a symptom of his loss of coherence. Since the fatherland is considered to be the primary source of identity, it is assumed that departure from it leads to the superimposition of a false self on the authentic self, whose gestures toward meaning in the new environment result only in further self-estrangement. Arrival in the United States represents self-denial on another level, for it implies that Cubans have renounced their national heritage and identified with the enemies of the fatherland:

Uno se siente más tranquilo
con Maceo allá arriba,
ardiendo en el gran sol de nuestra sangre,
que con Weyler, vertiéndola a sablazos.

[One feels more tranquil
with Maceo on high,
blazing in the big sun of our blood,
than with Weyler, shedding it with strokes from his saber.]

("La herencia," 2: 289)

The patriotic allusion, which links the Revolution with the Wars of Independence, causes emigration to appear as an act of betrayal. Moreover, it is suggested that in choosing to abandon the fatherland at a critical moment of its history, the exiles do more than simply impede the process of reconstruction by depriving the fatherland of their talents; they also express a refusal to participate in the national project of reappropriating an alienated heritage:

Sin embargo, no sé qué penetrante,
qué desasosegada
lástima me aprieta el corazón, pensando
en tus remotos descendientes,
dormidos en su gran noche previa,
su gran noche nonata.
Porque algún día imprevisible,
aún no establecido, pero cierto,
van a verse acosados
por la pregunta necesaria.
Tal vez en la clase de historia
algún camarada.
Acaso en una fábrica. La novia
pudiera ser. En cualquier sitio, en fin,
donde se hable de este hoy
que será para entonces un portentoso ayer.
Sabrán lo que es la herencia que les dejas,
esta especie de sífilis
que ahora testas con tu fuga,

[Nevertheless, I can't explain what a deep,
what a disturbing
pity seizes my heart, when thinking
of your distant descendants,
asleep in their big predestined darkness,
their big, unnaturally born night.
For on some unforeseeable day,
not yet appointed, but certain,
they are going to find themselves harassed
by the necessary question.

Perhaps in history class
a friend.
Maybe in a factory. It could be
the fiancée. In short, any place
where they talk about this today
which will be by then an extraordinary yesterday.
They will learn of the heritage that you leave them,
this kind of syphilis
that you now bequeath with your flight,]

(2: 287-88)

Absence from Cuba thus comes to appear as a willful form of self-mutilation in that it represents a renunciation of the national quest for wholeness. By rejecting the radiant center of Cuba for the dark night of the United States, the exiles condemn themselves and their descendants to a lifetime of incompleteness, of which their degraded speech is but a visible sign.

Nevertheless, if living in the United States is thought to establish a discontinuity in the consciousness and experience of all Cubans, it is considered to pose an even greater threat to the being of Afro-Cubans:

Un negro en Miami
no tiene casa donde vivir;
un negro en Miami
no tiene mesa donde comer;
un negro en Miami
no tiene cama donde dormir;
un negro en Miami
no tiene vaso donde beber,
si no es la casa,
si no es la mesa,
si no es la cama,
si no es el vaso
de un negro negro lo mismo que él.

[A black man in Miami
has no place to live;
a black man in Miami
has no place to eat;
a black man in Miami
has no place to sleep;
a black man in Miami
has no place to drink,
except in the house,
except at the table,
except in the bed,
except from the glass
of another black man as black as himself.]

("¡Ay, qué tristeza que tengo!," 2: 171-72)

Presumably, it is the nature of race relations in the American South that circumscribes the existence of Afro-Cubans. What Guillén fails to point out, however, is that other Cubans also contribute to the difficulties experienced by Afro-Cubans in Miami.[14] Yet, even as he calls into question the chances for survival of the Cuban self in exile, Guillén suggests that the process of adaptation will be less problematic for the bourgeoisie because their prerevolutionary lifestyle was so similar to the American way of life:

> Y de repente, Miami. Como si dijéramos La Habana
> que buscabas,
> tu Habana fácil y despreocupada.
> (Políticos baratos ¡que costaban tan caro!
> Burdeles, juego, yanquis, mariguana.)
> Magnífico.
>
> [And suddenly, Miami. As if we said that you were looking
> for Havana,
> your easy and relaxed Havana.
> (Cheap politicians, who cost so much!
> Brothels, gambling, Yankees, marijuana.)
> Fine.]

("La herencia," 2: 287)

In the case of blacks, on the other hand, emigration is considered to result in a more definitive state of homelessness, since in Miami they are denied both the material and spiritual benefits that were made available to them in revolutionary Cuba:

> Ay, qué tristeza que tengo,
> ay, qué tristeza tan grande,
> viendo correr a este negro
> sin que lo persiga nadie.
>
> Se asustó,
> parece que se asustó,
> de Cuba se fue, salió,
> llegó a Miami
> y allá en Miami se quedó.
> . . . .
>   —A Miami te fuiste un día,
>   vendiste tu libertad,
>   tu vergüenza y tu alegría,
>   yo sé que te pesará!
>
> [Oh, how sad I feel,
> oh, what a great sadness,
> on seeing this black man run
> without anybody pursuing him.

He got scared,
it seems that he got scared,
he went away from Cuba, he left,
he arrived in Miami
and there in Miami he stayed.
. . . .

> "One day you went away to Miami,
> you sold your freedom,
> your dignity and your joy,
> I know you will regret it!"]
>
> (" ¡Ay, qué tristeza que tengo!" 2: 171)

By indicating that fears about the course of events in Cuba are insufficient grounds to warrant the emigration of blacks to the United States, Guillén evidently subscribes to the popular view that blacks are the principal beneficiaries of the Revolution,[15] and as such, are ill-advised to abandon the system that endowed them with "freedom, dignity, and joy." The persistence of a differential perception of blacks and whites, even in a revolutionary situation, has caused several black scholars to be skeptical of the egalitarian postures of Cuba's revolutionary government.[16]

But, if one may borrow a phrase from Roberto Fernández Retamar, and define freedom as "consciously assuming the true condition of our history,"[17] then it appears from Guillén's poem, "Vine en un barco negrero" (I came on a Slave Ship), that to a certain extent, blacks in revolutionary Cuba are in a state of freedom. Unlike the protagonists of Guillén's early poems, who are generally dehumanized figures of fun, passive spectators of history, or entertainers of one sort or another, the persona of the poem is cast in a more heroic light by virtue of his association with exemplary figures from the past. The poem thus traces his constitution as a knowing subject as he progresses from being an object of manipulation by others: "me trajeron" (they brought me) (2: 106), to his arrival at a stage of greater awareness: "veo" (I see) (2: 107). Through his assumption of the experience of slave rebellions, the Wars of Independence, and the trade unionism of the 1940s, the character reflects a growing historical consciousness that is readily perceptible to the reader because of the dramatic structure of the poem. At the same time, the language that records the changes in his social condition also contains a psychological dimension. Thus, whereas the image of slavery is evoked by the phrase, "sudor como caramelo" (sweat like a caramel) (2: 106), a more dynamic register is chosen for portraying the struggle for Independence:

Pasó a caballo Maceo.
Yo en su séquito.
Largo el aullido del viento.
Alto el trueno.
Un fulgor de macheteros.
Yo con ellos.

[Maceo came on horseback.
I in his retinue.
Long the howl of the wind.
Loud the thunder.
A splendor of machete-wielders.
I with them.]

("Vine en un barco negrero. . . ," 2: 107)

The more positive sense of self projected by the persona has caused one critic to assert that in the poem, Guillén expresses pride in "who he has been and who he is today."[18] And indeed, in his willingness to treat slavery and Independence not as simply prehistorical phenomena, but as events whose course was affected by the intentional acts of Aponte and Maceo, Guillén does appear to take pride in "who he has been." Moreover, the statement, "Soy un negro" (I am a black man) (2: 108), seems to indicate a high degree of self-esteem. Yet, when the statement is situated in its context and regarded as a synthesized view of "who he is today," it fails to serve as an adequate comment on the contemporary situation, since the situation is perceived so schematically:

¡Oh Cuba! Mi voz entrego.
En ti creo.
Mía la tierra que beso.
Mío el cielo.

Libre estoy, vine de lejos.
Soy un negro.

[Oh Cuba! I submit my voice.
I believe in you.
Mine is the land that I kiss.
Mine the sky.

I am free, I came from afar.
I am a black man.]

(2: 108)

Even while freedom is being extolled, the persona, who presumably embodies the idea of freedom, is not placed in a position in which to exercise his new-found freedom. At the same time, as if to indicate their superfluousness in the present, no modern equivalent of Aponte, Maceo or Menéndez appears.

And yet, it has been noted that many of Guillén's revolutionary poems tend to "focus on the situation of blacks in the United States."[19] In fact, not only does Guillén express concern for the plight of the average black American, but he has also composed poetic tributes to Angela Davis and Martin Luther King. In Guillén's reluctance to portray contemporary Afro-Cubans in other than a conformist light, and in his writing of political activists in the United States, one perceives the well-known revolutionary contention that militancy is justified only in capitalist societies where private ownership of the means of production functions to maintain blacks in a subordinate position, as opposed to the situation in socialist societies, where militancy is unnecessary because all men have become brothers.[20] Thus, as in the poem, "K K K," racism appears to be a specifically American problem:

> Este cuadrúpedo procede
> de Joplin, Misurí.
> Carnicero.
> Aúlla largamente en la noche
> sin su dieta habitual de negro asado.
>
> Acabará por sucumbir.
> Un problema (*insoluble*) alimentarlo.
>
> [This quadruped comes from
> Joplin, Missouri.
> Butcher.
> He howls all night long
> without his steady diet of roasted blacks.
>
> He will end up by dying.
> An (*insoluble*) problem is feeding him.]

("K K K," 2: 239)

The note of optimism on which the poem ends derives from the assumption that racial equality has been achieved in Cuba through the measures adopted by the revolutionary government for institutionalizing equality. However, even if one chooses to ask, as does Carlos More, whether there is a place for blacks in revolutionary Cuba,[21] it should be stated that the political process that elicited poetic responses like Guillén's "Cualquier tiempo pasado fue peor" (All Past Time was Worse) reveals a public acknowledgement of the existence of racial discrimination in Cuba. In the words of Leslie Rout, when this public acknowledgement is seen in the context of Spanish-American race relations, it constitutes in itself a revolutionary act.[22]

Moreover, as Guillén indicates in the following epigram, racial inequality is embedded in the very fabric of the Spanish language:

Pienso:
¡Qué raro
que al tiro al blanco
no le hayan puesto *tiro al negro*!

[I think:
How strange
that they have not substituted
tiro al negro for target shooting!]

("*Epigramas*," 2: 327)[23]

"Negro" (black) cannot be readily substituted for "blanco" (white) without raising the specter of genocide. On the other hand, if the color component in the referential code of both terms is placed in parentheses, the attempt at transvaluation results in a loss of intelligibility.

The inquiry to which Guillén's epigram leads is not confined to the field of race relations, for the center/periphery dialectic also affects the area of international affairs. In everyday use of the idiom "tiro al blanco" (target shooting), the process by which "blanco" (white) becomes "target" remains concealed; similarly, in the following stanzas of the poem "Problemas del subdesarrollo" (Problems of Underdevelopment), the method by which particular states become inscribed in the center of the international community also remains hidden:

Monsieur Dupont te llama inculto,
porque ignoras cuál era el nieto
preferido de Víctor Hugo.

Herr Müller se ha puesto a gritar,
porque no sabes el día
(exacto) en que murió Bismarck.

Tu amigo Mr. Smith,
inglés o yanqui, yo no lo sé,
se subleva cuando escribes *shell*.
(Parece que ahorras una ele,
y que además pronuncias *chel*.)

[Monsieur Dupont calls you a savage,
because you do not know which was Victor Hugo's
favorite grandson.

Herr Müller has started screaming,
because you do not know the (exact) day
when Bismarck died.

Your friend, Mr. Smith,

Englishman or American, I am not sure,
has a fit when you write *shell*.
(It seems that you leave off one l,
and besides you pronounce it *chel*.)]

("Problemas del subdesarrollo," 2: 293)

Since the causes of effects are erased, what becomes visible are results
that are immobilized into absolute categories of value. In nations that
are situated on the periphery of the global community, historicity
withdraws from events that take place in the metropolis. Thus, when
specific items of knowledge about France or Germany lose their signs
of localization, they acquire the status of eternal truths. For the non-
European, absence from the place where the activities of Bismarck
acquire social significance, and the unidirectional flow of the information that he subsequently receives, emphasize his subordination to
the dispensers of enlightenment. His dependence is further dramatized
by the fact that he remains the same, even as they are differentiated
one from the other. Nevertheless, as the encounter with Mr. Smith
indicates, information from the metropolis is not poured into an
empty cultural space. Competing phonetic systems simply objectify
the existential condition of people in underdeveloped countries who
must retain local allegiances even as they are obliged to participate
in the affairs of the world at large.

It seems that for Guillén, centrality is simply a question of interchangeable linguistic signs. Hence he gives the following advice to his
imaginary listener:

Bueno ¿y qué?
Cuando te toque a ti,
mándales decir cacarajícara,
y que dónde está el Aconcagua,
y que quién era Sucre,
y que en qué lugar de este planeta
murió Martí.

Un favor:
que te hablen siempre en español.

[Well, and so what?
When it's your turn,
order them to say cacarajícara,
and ask where is the Aconcagua,
and who was Sucre,
and in what part of this planet
did Martí die.

One favor:
have them always speak to you in Spanish.]

(2: 293)

As the amended list of cultural phenomena reveals, what Guillén proposes is an insertion of Spanish-American references in the site previously occupied by Victor Hugo and company. Yet, except in the case of Martí, the list as it stands is merely a catalog of atemporal essences that give no indication of their human significance. National culture is here perceived as a predetermined repertoire of objects whose meaning is already an element of their structure, and thus no longer requires the mediation of active human agents to bring their social value into being. However, the degree of identification that the poem assumes with its implied audience suggests that interpretation is considered a less urgent task than the project of achieving cultural autonomy. But even if cultural ex-centricity is reflected in language, the "problems of underdevelopment" are not resolved by mere linguistic acts, for the phenomenon of cultural domination is only one dimension of a larger problem not readily visible in Guillén's text. Equally absent is the enabling mechanism that would bridge the gap between the present, when Monsieur Dupont exercises cultural initiative, and the anticipated moment "when it's your turn." In the face of the missing third term, the attempt to alter the existing asymmetrical arrangement in Spanish America's favor remains the expression of a desire, grounded on the verbal proposition, "mándales decir" (order them to say).

Undoubtedly, the desire to enter the mainstream of history was one of the causes of the Cuban Revolution. Yet, even as the revolutionary vanguard strove to assert their control over the course of events, they set in motion forces hostile to their definition of self-determination. Guillén's poems on the blockade, the Bay of Pigs incident, and the Missile Crisis record some of the obstacles faced by the Cuban leadership in the international sphere, while "Balada" (Ballad) indicates that the consolidation of power within Cuba itself has required the crushing of forces actively opposed to the regime. If the list of fallen heroes like Conrado Benítez and Camilo Cienfuegos serves as a convenient focus for expressions of solidarity, it also emphasizes the high cost of revolutionary struggle.

While there is no doubt that Guillén supports the general principles of the Revolution, it is also clear that he is well aware of some of its limitations. In the following epigram, for example, he comments on the instant mobility achieved by those who chose to remain in Cuba and were thrust into positions of responsibility for which they were ill-prepared:[24]

Maravillan
las cosas que hay en este mundo:
ese muchacho zurdo

dejó el abecedario
para enseñar filosofía.

[This is
indeed a strange world:
that left-handed kid
quit the alphabet
in order to teach philosophy.]

("Epigramas," 2:328)

At the same time, there is also a recognition on Guillén's part of some of the more problematic aspects of the effort to build socialism in Cuba:

Está el tenor en éxtasis
contemplando al tenor
del espejo, que es el mismo tenor
en éxtasis
que contempla al tenor.

Sale a veces a pasear por el mundo
llevado de un bramante de seda,
aplaudido en dólares,
tinta de imprenta
y otras sustancias gananciales.
(Aquí en el Zoo le molesta
cantar por la comida
y no es muy generoso con sus arias.)
Milán Scala.
New York Metropolitan.
Ópera de París.

[The tenor is in ecstasy
beholding the tenor
in the mirror, who is the same tenor
in ecstasy
beholding the tenor.

Sometimes he travels around the world
led by a silk thread,
applauded in dollars,
printer's ink
and other profitable substances.
(Here in the Zoo it bothers him
to sing for his supper
and he is not very generous with his arias.)
Milan, La Scala.
The New York Metropolitan.
The Paris Opera.]

("Tenor," 2: 242-43)

The parenthetical comment by Guillén, the tour guide, brings into focus the lack of congruence between the collectivizing intentions of the regime and individual modes of behavior that frustrate the realization of those intentions. Guillén's satiric tone makes even more evident the fact that in an economy of scarcity, where artists are expected to be motivated by altruism, the willed separation between individual effort and personal reward often fails to produce the desired results. Instead of leading to a heightened sense of identification between tenor and society, the expectation that the tenor subordinate his talents to the needs of the community results in the disengagement of the artist from the very society he is supposed to serve. An exaggerated degree of self-centeredness is only part of the problem. A more fundamental issue is that for the tenor the locus of value is situated on the far side of the cage, where artistic success is measured in materialistic terms. Thus, restrictions on his mobility fail to make him a more contented and productive worker.

It was against such residual expressions of bourgeois egoism that the Revolutionary Offensive was launched in 1968.[25] The logical result was a call for greater ideological purity. In the face of the mounting insistence on orthodoxy, Guillén's reaction was the poem, "Digo que yo no soy un hombre puro" (I say that I am not a pure man):

Yo no voy a decirte que soy un hombre puro.
Entre otras cosas
falta saber si es que lo puro existe.
O si es, pongamos, necesario.
O posible,
O si sabe bien.

[I am not going to tell you that I am a pure man.
Among other things
it is necessary to find out if purity exists.
Or if it is, let's say, necessary.
Or possible.
Or if it tastes good.]

("Digo que yo no soy un hombre puro," 2: 297)

Guillén's critique was evidently motivated by a desire to see the revolutionary system function more effectively. He is careful to project his criticism from "within the Revolution" and not exceed its permissible limits by supporting such counterrevolutionary vices as homosexuality:

Yo no te digo pues que soy un hombre puro,
yo no te digo eso, sino todo lo contrario.

Que amo (a las mujeres, naturalmente,
pues mi amor puede decir su nombre),
y me gusta comer carne de puerco con papas,
. . . .
Soy impuro ¿qué quieres que te diga?
Completamente impuro.
Sin embargo,
creo que hay muchas cosas puras en el mundo
que no son más que pura mierda.

[I am not telling you that I am a pure man,
I am not saying that, but quite the opposite.
That I love (women, naturally,
since my love can voice her name),
and I like to eat pork and potatoes,
. . . .
I am impure, what do you want me to say?
Completely impure.
However,
I believe there are many pure things in the world
that are only pure shit.]

(2: 297)

Perhaps part of the difficulty in establishing a socialist paradise in Cuba lies in the fact that socialism has yet to be presented in consistently positive terms. In other words, instead of being presented as a state to be striven *for*, socialism is often defined *against* a competing ideological system. Richard Fagen has already examined the predominance of negative images of the future during the early phases of the Revolution and pointed out the critical importance of "the enemy" for crystallizing popular enthusiasm in the revolutionary situation.[26] Nevertheless, in Guillén's "Unión Soviética" (Soviet Union), the friend, so crucial for the survival of the revolutionary effort in Cuba, is virtually engulfed by the enemy, who is indeed the absent center of the text:

Jámas he visto un trust soviético en mi patria.
Ni un banco.
Ni tampoco un ten cents.
Ni un central.
Ni una estación naval.
Ni un tren.
Nunca jamás hallé
un campo de bananas
donde al pasar leyera
"Máslov and Company, S. en C.
Plátanos al por mayor. Oficinas en Cuba:
Maceo esquina con No-sé-qué."

[I have never seen a Soviet trust in my country.
Nor a bank.
Nor a dime store either.
Nor a sugar factory.
Nor a naval station.
Nor a train.
I never passed by
a banana field
where it said:
"Maslov and Company, Ltd.
Wholesale bananas. Cuban Office:
Corner of Maceo and Such-and-Such-A-Street."]

("Unión Soviética," 2: 93)

Admittedly, Cuba's proximity to the United States, and the degree of American involvement in Cuba before the Revolution, help to explain the continued perception of the United States as an overwhelming presence in revolutionary Cuba. Moreover, the geopolitical consequences of the Revolution cause the United States to play a silent but important role in the daily affairs of revolutionary Cuba.[27] Thus, even when a positive reference is made to the Soviet Union in Guillén's poem, it appears in the form of a reply to a hypothetical question posed by the enemy:

En nuestro mar nunca encontré
piratas de Moscú.
(Hable, Caribe, usted.)
Ni de Moscú tampoco en mis claras bahías
ese ojo-radar superatento
las noches y los días
queriendo adivinar mi pensamiento.
Ni bloqueos.
Ni marines.
Ni lanchas para infiltrar espías.
¿Barcos soviéticos? Muy bien.
Son petroleros, mire usted.
Son pescadores, sí, señor.
Otros llevan azúcar, traen café
junto a fragantes ramos de esperanzas en flor.

[In our sea I never found
pirates from Moscow.
(Speak, Caribbean.)
Nor from Moscow in my clear bays
that superattentive radar-eye
night and day
wishing to guess my thoughts.
Nor blockades.
Nor marines.

Nor boats for infiltrating spies.
Soviet ships? Very well.
They are oil tankers, see.
They are fishing boats, yes, sir.
Others carry sugar, bring coffee
as well as fragrant branches of hope in flower.]

(2: 94)

It is this explicitly committed stance in Guillén's revolutionary poems that has earned them a negative evaluation from critics like Lourdes Casal.[28] Yet, poems like "El cangrejo" (Cancer) and "Bomba atómica" (Atomic Bomb) indicate that Guillén is concerned not only about the survival of the Cuban Revolution, but also about the fate of man and society in general. Moreover, while poems like "Tengo" (I have) and "¿Puedes?" (Can You?) express unqualified support for the utopian aims of the Revolution, "Digo que yo no soy un hombre puro" (I say that I am not a pure man) criticizes the Revolution's extremism, and "Tenor" raises doubts about the prospects for the birth of "the new socialist man" in a climate of political isolation. On the other hand, as Keith Ellis has observed, social poetry like Guillén's, which Lourdes Casal seeks to bracket and thereby preclude from serious consideration, has been a marked characteristic of Cuban literature in particular, and of Latin American literature in general, since their early beginnings.[29] Consequently, Guillén's endorsement of the revolutionary belief in the perfectibility of man and society is simply another contribution to this poetic tradition.

CONCLUSION

My analysis of Guillén's work is based on the premise that the poet's creative work forms a coherent body of expression. Because Guillén's poetry is referential in nature, the context in which his words were uttered had to be considered. It was necessary to examine Guillén's use of language in order to understand the way in which the poet came to terms with the African dimension of his own being in light of prevailing concepts of Africa. Similarly, in order to appreciate fully the normative thrust of the poet's perceptions about the relationship between self and society, it was necessary to analyze the ideological assumptions of the Marxist philosophy to which he subscribed, and to bear in mind the activities of the Castro government that he served.

Because the poet's language was firmly anchored in a social context, it was necessary to consider sociopolitical issues for which certain poems attempted to provide a solution. The divided self of the Afro-Cuban, the irresponsibility of national leaders, militarism, and American domination of Latin America were all seen by Guillén as fitting themes for poetry. This phenomenon is in keeping with the idealistic thrust of Latin American literature, for the critique of society and proposals for a better world have been recurrent themes in a continent where the writer has traditionally perceived his role to be that of serving as the conscience of his people.[1]

Ethical engagement with his fellow men led Guillén to give his verses a particular form of expression. The early poems, for example, attempt to transcend their written condition and to attain the quality of the spoken word. Later poems in which Guillén treats well-known events and the frequent use of dialogue also attest to Guillén's effort to restore the sound of the human voice to the printed word. Guillén's early poems, which take up the question of an Afro-Cuban identity, exemplify the emphasis on orality in its most exaggerated form, for they approximate typographically the sounds of spontaneous speech. But, as the poems supposedly addressed to the military indicate, even when the effort to effect a merger between sight and sound is less explicit, the oral aspect is still retained.

The emphasis on verbal performance stems from the normative thrust of Guillén's poetry. In an attempt to create a national consciousness among his readers, Guillén frequently cast his poems in a declamatory mode so as to induce in his readers an awareness of the shortcomings of the polity in which they lived and to encourage in them a willingness to act to remedy the perceived ills. For it was felt that once Cuba was freed from Spanish domination and became incorporated into the American sphere of influence, the original expectation that the movement for independence would result in a nation that embodied the ideals of all segments of the population was a failed project.

Admittedly, the process by which Cuba arrived at nationhood was felt to have an inhibiting effect on the Cuban capacity for self-definition. Despite the constitutional changes, the sociopolitical institutions that were created to serve the new nation were modeled on American concepts of good government. Because political leaders were less concerned with furthering the interests of their constituents than with maintaining a semblance of order under the watchful eyes of the United States, the institutions ostensibly charged with coordinating national affairs failed to function effectively. Inasmuch as the United States failed to recognize the freedom of Cubans, Cubans were considered to have an inaccurate view of themselves because their knowledge of themselves was affected by their relationship to the more powerful and alien others.

What was felt to be lacking was a coherent social philosophy that gave all members of the young nation a sense of shared values. The problem of finding a locus of social cohesion was compounded by the fact that early republican Cuba continued to be a segmented society. Slavery had existed within recent memory, and it was difficult for the members of the ruling groups to articulate a national consciousness in a society where ethnicity still served as a primary marker of common identity. Moreover, the importing of Haitian and Jamaican laborers to perform the menial tasks of the sugar plantation that Cubans were reluctant to assume helped to perpetuate the racial division of labor that had been in effect since the sixteenth century.

While the government's attempts to limit the stay of the non-Hispanic workers in Cuba could be seen as an effort to maintain the cultural unity of the island, the importation of agricultural workers did little to convince the native Afro-Cuban that he had a role to play in the nationalist project. At the same time, caution was considered to be advisable because a movement to seek political redress, led by disgruntled veterans of the Wars of Independence, had been brutally suppressed in 1912. When the sugar market collapsed in the 1920s and the entire economy was thrown into disarray, black marginality became more pronounced than ever. Self-acceptance became problematic for blacks; although it was said that they were the equals of all other citizens of the republic, they had limited social opportunities. Belief in the Afro-Cuban's ability to shape his own circumstances was undermined by the constraints upon his freedom to act.

However, simple economic explanations for the black condition proved inadequate in a situation where social divisions seemed to coincide with ethnic affiliation. In some instances, a superfluous existence was attributed to personal shortcomings. But, in such cases, the locus of self-appraisal was often outside the self. Blacks who were dissatisfied with their physical appearance because it was held to be the primary cause of their deteriorating economic condition had taken up the attitudes that the other members of the society had toward them. Those who consciously strove to alter their appearance were equally self-estranged, for once they had internalized alien concepts of an ideal self, their efforts at personal transformation were unlikely to render them as aesthetically pleasing subjects in their own eyes. Cosmetic changes would merely serve to indicate the distance that separated them from their physical ideal.

On the other hand, the affirmation of an ethnic consciousness in a society that perceived itself to be a harmonious fusion of disparate elements had already proved to be dangerous, and adherents were punished by persecution and death. At the same time, the more conspicuous signs of ethnicity were often manipulated by opportunistic politicians who sought to advance their careers through the votes of the sizable black population.[2]

When the cultivation of ethnicity became a respectable pastime during the 1920s, thanks to European interest in the primitive, Cuban writers participated in the international movement by offering stylized treatments of black dancers and of Afro-Cuban religious ceremonies. Paradoxically, the internationalist tendency to exalt black sensuality was perceived as a national mode of expression.[3] Yet, it was essentially the work of alienated intellectuals who had been declassed by the economic upheavals of the 1920s and who, from their position on the fringes of their society, were seeking to exert a restraining influence on what was regarded as the materialistic excesses of the young republic.[4] Their exclusion from the center of power was felt as a betrayal of the ideals of independence and resulted in a quest for the "true" national essence. The symbolic embrace of Afro-Cuban culture became an integral part of that quest, inasmuch as it seemed to herald the movement from a position of marginality to one of centrality. Nevertheless, *negrismo* yielded few visions of authenticity because its predominant focus on the picturesque failed to reveal the human dimension of the black existence that it sought to evoke. The ironic treatment of Afro-Cuban culture pointed to racial polarity rather than to cultural synthesis.

Guillén was one of the few writers of his generation who was not content to view the Afro-Cuban as an exotic fragment of African man; he viewed the Afro-Cuban, rather, as an autonomous being who lived the contradictions of his Caribbean homeland. Sustained detachment from the situation was probably impossible for Guillén because, as a mulatto, he embodied the American's attempt to assimilate elements of the European and African cultures. Thus, Guillén sought to go beyond the fragmented images of the Afro-Cuban that were offered by most of his peers, as well as by Guillén himself at the beginning of his career. The abject conditions in which many of the poet's black characters were shown to exist thus came to be seen not as testimony of the animalistic nature of blacks, nor as the result of the black man's cheerful indifference to his material well-being, but as a consequence of the fundamental problems of the polity. If blacks lived in overcrowded tenements, that was less a sign of promiscuity than of the economic stagnation of the larger society. If Afro-Cubans seemed to live only in the eternal present, they were simply expressing the fatalism of many Cubans who, in the light of the Platt Amendment to the Cuban Constitution, had come to feel that they had little control over the internal development of their island.

So pervasive was the Cuban feeling of powerlessness that even the acknowledged leaders of the nation had little sense of themselves as causal agents. Although they were nominally responsible for guiding the affairs of the nation, they too had a sense of being alienated from their own history. Unconvinced of their capacity to rule, the leaders of early republican Cuba often made no attempt to solve the problems that they faced and were quite willing to leave that responsibility to others. What should have been perceived as national issues was thereby reduced to the level of the personal, inasmuch as specific actions often lacked a broader social purpose. Party switching, for example, took place not for ideological reasons but whenever it was felt to be personally more advantageous to do so. At the same time, the consequence of such actions upon the political structure of the nation was not taken into account.[5]

Since the United States was always willing to intervene whenever the political stability of the island was felt to be threatened, the official boundaries of the state existed only in principle. The inability, or unwillingness, of Cubans to protect their island from engulfment by its more powerful neighbor was reproduced at the level of interpersonal relations in that the boundaries between self and other came to be equally fluid. Being Cuban and being American ceased to be experienced as separate and distinct processes because American recognition began to be considered important for providing the Cuban with the stable core that he was felt to lack. By appropriating selected aspects of American behavior, Cubans attempted to overcome their feeling of internal fragmentation and to achieve a sense of coherence and national purpose. But in resorting to an alien mode of being as the means for bolstering their faltering sense of identity, they succeeded only in undermining even further their belief in the efficacy of their own conduct.

The devaluation of self inherent in the Cuban assumption of American patterns of behavior is harshly censured by Guillén because it is seen as a perpetuation of the colonial condition that Cubans had presumably repudiated when they initiated the struggle for political independence from Spain. The poet is particularly critical of the use of English by Cubans to articulate their desires since the spoken language was seen as an index of the extent to which Cubans had become alienated from their own cultural standards. Guillén therefore exposes Cuban mimetic behavior to ridicule in order to indicate the need for a more positive interaction between Cubans and their environment.

But if Cubans were as hopelessly colonized as Guillén seems to imply in moments of despair, then the poetic articulation of the prospect of self-realization would be an exercise in futility. The experience of slavery, as well as Cuba's situation first as a Spanish colony and later as a dependency of the United States, would have predisposed Cubans to an existence of secondariness. Eternally separated from the sources of their authenticity because of their political and economic circumstances, Cubans would be condemned to perpetuate their alienation since their history of subordination would mean that they lacked the inner resources for transforming their condition of dependency into one of autonomy.

However, while such a view of the Cuban self was understandable during the 1930s, when political instability, militarism, and the stagnation of a one-crop economy made the average Cuban painfully aware of the gap between his desire for social transformation and the structural limitations upon his ability to effect the changes desired, it does not represent the full scope of Guillén's perceptions of the Cuban situation. While the poet recognizes the existence of objective constraints upon the individual's freedom to act, the fact that many of his poems point to an alternative vision of the self in society indicates his belief that human behavior was not completely determined by external circumstances. Once intentionality is attributed to socio-political forces and man is considered to be a helpless victim, not only is the path to future change blocked, but the continuous efforts made by Cubans over the centuries to shape their environment would be emptied of historical meaning. Guillén's focus on the exploits of rebellious slaves, nineteenth-century patriots, and twentieth-century leaders is clearly an attempt to establish cultural continuity, which makes the Castro revolution appear to be the latest effort on the part of Cubans to define their own existence.

If the United States seemed to threaten Cuba with denationaliza-tion, its actions provided an opportunity for Guillén to reestablish the boundaries between both cultures, and thereby remind his Cuban readers that they are radically different from Americans and that they have common ties with each other. In his aim to create a national consciousness, Guillén hoped to see an end to American hegemony in Cuba, and by extension, in all of Latin America. He also hoped that the negation of American influence would result in a more socially harmonious mode of existence. A society where race and class were no longer categories of value, where all would be adequately housed and fed, where work would be a creative act, and where man would recognize his mutuality with his neighbor was seen by Guillén as the goal to which Cuba should aspire. And while Guillén was aware that powerful forces within and outside Cuba would be opposed to the realization of social justice in the island, his belief that authentic self-expression was otherwise impossible led him to posit the necessity of striving for an equitable society.

Long before the Castro regime came into existence, Guillén advo-cated the need to restructure Cuban society so that all Cubans could achieve fulfillment as human beings. As was mentioned earlier, Guillén's position derives in part from his situating himself as a writer within the utopian tradition of Latin American literature. It also stems from his espousal of Marxist philosophy, although his belief in the Marxist ideal of the classless society leads him to go beyond the expected denunciation of the condition of the oppressed and to place them at the center of his vision through the linguistic representation of their speech and gestures. Presumably, the symbolic overcoming of social divisions embodied in the poetry would inspire readers to effect similar changes in the empirical world. Yet, more than twenty years would elapse before a concrete attempt would be made to create the egalitarian society envisaged by Guillén.

Since many of the new government's policies coincided with the

poet's views of the relationship between man and society, Guillén
expressed his approval of the changes implemented in several verses.
But support for the regime did not blind Guillén either to its failings
or to the difficulties of the historical task it had set for itself. However,
the tone of restraint that characterizes the poet's criticisms of the
revolutionary government contrasts markedly with the vituperative
language used to censure the shortcomings of earlier republican governments. This raises therefore the interesting question of whether Guillén's subdued tone, as far as the failings of revolutionary Cuba are
concerned, was the logical result of his official position as president
of the National Writers' Union, or whether it corresponds objectively
to his view that, despite its shortcomings, the new Cuba has succeeded
in giving all Cubans a sense of belonging to the nation for the first
time in the island's history.[6]

NOTES

Chapter 1

1. Guillén was the son of a newspaper editor and Liberal senator who had fought in the Second War of Independence and was killed in a political skirmish in 1917. In 1920, Guillén left his native city of Camagüey to study law at the University of Havana, but, bored by his studies, he decided to become a full-time poet instead. While in Havana, he witnessed the sociopolitcal struggles that resulted in the overthrow of President Gerardo Machado in 1933. The political ascendancy of the military in the wake of Machado's overthrow affected Guillén personally when he was jailed in 1936 for being on the editorial board of a leftist journal that was accused by the government of publishing "subversive propaganda." In 1937 he traveled to war-torn Spain as a delegate to the International Congress for the Defense of Culture. For biographical details through 1948, see Ángel Augier, *Nicolás Guillén: Notas para un estudio biográfico-crítico*, 2 vols. (Havana: Universidad Central de Las Villas, 1964). For a brief updated account of Guillén's life, see Robert Márquez, "Introduction," *¡Patria o Muerte! The Great Zoo and Other Poems by Nicolás Guillén* (New York: Monthly Review Press, 1972), pp. 13-28.

2. Even though Guillén did not participate actively in the struggle against Batista, his work is considered revolutionary by the Castro government, particularly his *Cantos para soldados y sones para turistas* (Songs for Soldiers and Ballads for Tourists) (Mexico: Editorial Masas, 1937).

3. Cintio Vitier, *Lo cubano en la poesía* (Havana: Instituto del Libro, 1970), p. 420. The *son* was an Afro-Cuban dance rhythm popular in the Cuban countryside at the beginning of the century. Although it originally lacked prestige and was considered to be vulgar by the Cuban middle class, it gained greater social acceptance when a musical group, the Sexteto Habanero, incorporated it into their repertoire of dance music for Havana audiences during the 1920s. Like most black music, the *son* is structured on the call-and-response pattern, with a primary focus on rhythm and the predominance of percussion instruments. It is these formal aspects of the *son* that Guillén sought to capture in his early poetry. For further details on the structure of the *son*, see Dellita Martin Lowery, "Selected Poems of Nicolás Guillén and Langston Hughes: Their Use of Afro-Western Folk Music Genres" (Ph.D. diss., Ohio State University, 1975), pp. 51-53.

4. Vitier, *Lo cubano*, pp. 432-34.

5. Emir Rodríguez Monegal, ed., *The Borzoi Anthology of Latin American Literature* (New York: Alfred A. Knopf, 1977), 2: 609.

6. Arturo Torres-Ríoseco, *The Epic of Latin American Literature* (New York: Oxford University Press, 1942), p. 129.

7. Janheinz Jahn, *Muntu: An Outline of the New African Culture*, trans. Marjorie Grene (New York: Grove Press, 1961), p. 92.

8. Vitier, *Lo cubano*, pp. 420-21, 425-30.

9. Jahn, *Muntu*, pp. 92-95, 205-08.

10. See Wilfred G. Cartey, *Black Images* (New York: Teacher's College Press, 1970), pp. 15-28; G. R. Coulthard, *Race and Colour in Caribbean Literature* (London: Oxford University Press, 1962), pp. 27-30; Dennis Sardinha, "Cuba—The 'Negrista' Movement in the Process of National Integration," *Bim* 15 (June 1975): 110-17.

11. See José Juan Arrom, "La poesía afrocubana," in *Estudios de Literatura Hispanoamericana* (Havana: Úcar García, 1950), pp. 109-45; Dorothy Feldman Harth, "La poesía afrocubana, sus raíces e influencias," in *Miscelánea de estudios dedicados a Fernando Ortiz* (Havana: Úcar García, 1956), 3: 789-827; Mónica Mansour, *La poesía negrista* (Mexico: Ediciones Era, 1973), pp. 142-91; Rosa E. Valdés-Cruz, *La poesía negroide en América* (New York: Las Américas Publishing Co., 1970), pp. 21-33, 51-77.

12. Cf. Emilio Ballagas, "El mensaje inédito," in *Recopilación de textos sobre Nicolás Guillén*, ed. Nancy Morejón (Havana: Casa de las Américas, 1974), pp. 259-61; Alberto Lamar Schweyer, "La musa mulata," Ibid., pp. 255-58; Ezequiel Martínez Estrada, *La poesía afrocubana de Nicolás Guillén* (Montevideo: Editorial Arca, 1966).

13. Cited in Augier, *Notas*, 1: 121-22; Keith Ellis, "Nicolás Guillén at Seventy," *Caribbean Quarterly* 19 (March 1973): 88.

14. Cf. William W. Megenney, "Las cualidades afrocubanas en la poesía de Nicolás Guillén," *La Torre* 18 (July-September 1970): 127-38; Adriana Tous, *La poesía de Nicolás Guillén* (Madrid: Ediciones Cultura Hispánica, 1971), pp. 84-91, 114-45.

15. Lemuel A. Johnson, *The Devil, the Gargoyle, and the Buffoon: The Negro as Metaphor in Western Literature* (Port Washington, N.Y.: Kennikat Press, 1971), pp. 66-79.

16. Gordon Brotherston, *Latin American Poetry: Origins and Presence* (Cambridge: At the University Press, 1975), pp. 20-23.

17. See Roberto Márquez, "De rosa armado y de acero: La obra de Nicolás Guillén," *Sin Nombre* 4 (October-December 1973): 23-32; Ildefonso Pereda Valdés, *Lo negro y lo mulato en la poesía cubana* (Montevideo: Ediciones Ciudadela, 1970), pp. 55-82.

18. Jorge María Ruscalleda Bercedóniz, *La poesía de Nicolás Guillén (cuatro elementos sustanciales)* (Río Piedras, Puerto Rico: Editorial Universitaria, 1975).

19. See Roberto Fernández Retamar, *El son de vuelo popular* (Havana: Instituto Cubano del Libro, 1972); Alfred Melon, *Realidad, poesía e ideología* (Havana: Ediciones Unión, 1973); Nancy Morejón, "Prólogo," *Recopilación de textos sobre Nicolás Guillén*, pp. 7-29; Manuel Navarro Luna, "Un líder de la poesía revolucionaria," in Morejón, *Recopilación de textos*, pp. 101-15.

20. Juan Marinello, "Hazaña y triunfo americanos de Nicolás Guillén," in Morejón, *Recopilación de textos*, pp. 283-91.

21. See Augier, *Notas*, 1: 195-213, 2: 11-20, 30-101.

22. Lourdes Casal, "Literature and Society," in *Revolutionary Change in Cuba*, ed. Carmelo Mesa-Lago (Pittsburgh: University of Pittsburgh Press, 1971), p. 465.

23. José Antonio Portuondo, "Canta a la revolución con toda la voz que tiene," in Morejón, *Recopilación de textos*, pp. 303-09.

24. See Richard J. Carr, *Tengo* (Detroit: Broadside Press, 1974).

25. Robert Márquez and David Arthur McMurray, *Man-Making Words* (Amherst: University of Massachusetts Press, 1972); Robert Márquez, *The Great Zoo*.

26. Mirta Aguirre, "Maestro de poesía," in Morejón, *Recopilación de textos*, pp. 165-70.

27. Sylvia Wynter, "Ethno or Socio Poetics," in *Alcheringa: Ethnopoetics*, ed. Michel Benamou and Jerome Rothenberg (Boston: Boston University Press, 1976), pp. 79-94.

28. Fernández Retamar, *El son de vuelo popular*, pp. 38-89.

29. Lowery, "Selected Poems," pp. 2-138, 251-62. Cf. Arturo Sánchez-Rojas, "Papá Montero: Del son original al poema de Nicolás Guillén," *Caribe* (University of Hawaii) 5 (Fall 1976): 49-56.

30. Keith Ellis, "Literary Americanism and the Recent Poetry of Nicolás Guillén," *University of Toronto Quarterly* 45 (Fall 1975): 11-12.

31. Lowery cites illiteracy as the main factor impeding the free flow of information in Cuba during the 1930s. See "Selected Poems," pp. 125-27. Given the high rate of literacy in the Cuban population at that time, censorship was undoubtedly the more important reason. See Augier, *Notas*, 2: 13-19.

32. Ángel Augier, "La revolución cubana en la poesía de Nicolás Guillén," *Plural* 59 (August 1976): 47-61.

33. Melon, *Realidad, poesía e ideología*, pp. 27-28, 43-51.

34. Keith Ellis, "Literary Americanism," p. 12.

35. Melon, *Realidad, poesía e ideología*, pp. 49-55.

36. Ibid., pp. 25-42.

37. See, for example, Donald W. Bray and Timothy F. Harding, "Cuba," in *Latin America: The Struggle with Dependency and Beyond*, ed. Ronald H. Chilcote and Joel C. Edelstein (Cambridge, Mass.: Schenkman Publishing Co., 1974), pp. 579-604.

38. Cf. in Chilcote and Edelstein, eds., "Introduction," *Latin America*, pp. 24-46.

Chapter 2

1. M. G. Smith, "The African Heritage in the Caribbean," *Caribbean Studies: A Symposium*, ed. Vera Rubin (Seattle: University of Washington Press, 1960), p. 40.

2. Citations are from Nicolás Guillén, *Obra poética, 1920-1972*, 2 vols. (Havana: Instituto Cubano del Libro, 1974), and are given in the text parenthetically. All translations are by the author.

3. Regarding Yoruba supremacy in Cuba, see Salvador Bueno, "'La canción del bongó': Sobre la cultura mulata de Cuba," *Cuadernos Americanos* 206 (May-June 1976): 97.

4. For Shango's attributes, see William Bascom, *Shango in the New World* (Austin: University of Texas Press, 1972), pp. 14-15.

5. On the necessity of feeding the god, so as to transmit his protective power to the worshipper, see William Bascom, "The Focus of Cuban Santería," in *Peoples and Cultures of the Caribbean*, ed. Michael M. Horowitz (Garden City, N.Y.: The Natural History Press, 1971), pp. 523-25. Regarding the need for protective charms to be recharged periodically, see John S. Mbiti, *African Religions and Philosophy* (New York: Frederick A. Praeger, 1969), p. 199.

6. Mbiti, *African Religions*, p. 77.

7. On the mystical power of the word, Ibid., p. 197.

8. For the idea that African music is conceived vocally, see John Storm Roberts, *Black Music of Two Worlds* (New York: William Morrow and Co., 1974), p. 6. For the stylistic features of African music, see Richard Alan Waterman, "African Influence on the Music of the Americas," in *Acculturation in the Americas*, ed. Sol Tax (New York: Cooper Square Publishers, 1967), pp. 207-18.

9. Ruth Finnegan, *Oral Literature in Africa* (London: Oxford University Press, 1970), p. 265.

10. Coulthard, *Race and Colour*, pp. 27-29.

11. O. R. Dathorne, *The Black Mind: A History of African Literature* (Minneapolis: University of Minnesota Press, 1974), pp. 437-40.

12. Cf. Christopher Fyfe, "The Dynamics of African Dispersal: The Transatlantic Slave Trade," in *The African Diaspora: Interpretive Essays* ed. Martin L. Kilson and Robert I. Rotberg (Cambridge, Mass.: Harvard University Press, 1976), pp. 57-74; Joseph C. Miller, "The Slave Trade in Congo and Angola," ibid., pp. 75-113; G. J. Afolabi Ojo, *Yoruba Culture: A Geographical Analysis* (London: London University Press, 1966), pp. 108-22; Walter Rodney, "African Slavery and Other Forms of Social Oppression on the Upper Guinea Coast in the Context of the Atlantic Slave-Trade," *The Journal of African History* 7 (1966): 431-43; idem, *West Africa and the Atlantic Slave-Trade* (Nairobi: East African Publishing House, 1969).

13. Lloyd King, "Mr. Black in Cuba," *African Studies of the West Indies Bulletin* 5 (1972): 25-26.

14. Edward Kamau Brathwaite, "The African Presence in Caribbean Literature," in *Slavery, Colonialism, and Racism*, ed. Sidney W. Mintz (New York: W. W. Norton and Co., 1974), pp. 80-82.

15. Fernando Ortiz, *Hampa afro-cubana: Los negros brujos (apuntes para un estudio de etnología criminal)* (Madrid: Editorial América, 1917), p. 353. For an analysis of Cuba's late development as a plantation society, which would explain the presence of native Africans there in the twentieth century, see Franklin W. Knight, *Slave Society in Cuba in the Nineteenth Century* (Madison: University of Wisconsin Press, 1970).

16. George Lamming, "Actitudes de la literatura antillana con respecto a Africa," *Casa de las Américas* 56 (September-October 1969): 120-25.

17. George Lamming, *The Pleasures of Exile* (London: Michael Joseph, 1960), p. 160.

18. My italics.

19. Lamming, *Exile*, p. 160.

20. Roberts, *Black Music*, pp. 95-96.

21. Olabiyi Yai, "Influence yoruba dans la poésie cubaine: Nicolás Guillén et la tradition poétique yoruba" (Seminar Paper, Dept. of Modern European Languages, University of Ife, Nigeria, 1974-75), pp. 14-15. I am indebted to Maureen Warner-Lewis for providing me with a copy of this paper.

22. Finnegan, *Oral Literature*, p. 131.

23. Ibid., pp. 92-96.

24. Frantz Fanon, *The Wretched of the Earth*, trans. Constance Farrington (New York: Grove Press, 1963), pp. 38-40.

25. Ibid., p. 132.

26. René Depestre, "Los fundamentos socioculturales de nuestra identidad," *Casa de las Américas* 58 (January-February 1970): 27.

27. Kenneth W. Grundy, *Guerrilla Struggle in Africa: An Analysis and Preview* (New York: Grossman Publishers, 1971), pp. 78-79.

28. Antonio Olliz Boyd, "The Concept of Black Awareness as a Thematic Approach in Latin American Literature," in *Blacks in Hispanic Literature: Critical Essays*, ed. Miriam DeCosta (Port Washington, N.Y.: Kennikat Press, 1977), p. 66.

29. Fanon, *The Wretched*, p. 42.

Chapter 3

1. The first blacks arrived in Cuba from Spain around 1511. Few new arrivals came to settle on the island after Cuba lost its importance to the Spanish-American mainland and became a small ranching society. The island's emergence as a

major sugar producer in the late eighteenth century led to an influx of African laborers. By then, most nations were turning away from slave labor. The signing of the Anglo-Spanish treaty, in 1817, outlawing the slave trade, meant that the majority of slaves who arrived in the island between 1820, when the law went into effect, and 1866, when slave traffic finally ended, arrived illegally. For further details, see Knight, *Slave Society*, pp. 4-13, 22-35, 47-58.

2. Even though individual slaves could obtain their freedom in a variety of ways, slavery as an institution was abolished in stages in Cuba, beginning with the First War of Independence in 1868, when some slaves were freed by rebel plantation owners, and ending with the final decree of abolition in 1886. For an analysis of the factors leading to emancipation, see Knight, *Slave Society*, pp. 91-100, 137-78.

3. Frantz Fanon, *Black Skin, White Masks*, trans. Charles Lam Markmann (New York: Grove Press, 1967), pp. 11-14.

4. *Adelantá* (light) derives from *adelantar*, which means "to advance," "to improve."

5. The term is used by Hoetink to refer to the high social value placed on caucasoid physical features by dark-skinned peoples living in segmented societies. See H. Hoetink, *Caribbean Race Relations: A Study of Two Variants*, trans. Eva M. Hooykaas (London: Oxford University Press, 1971), pp. 120-90.

6. Lowery, "Selected Poems," pp. 74-75.

7. According to Fernando Ortiz, the word is derived from a West African term, *abombo*, which originally meant "nose." Through a process of association, it eventually came to refer to the protruding lips of the Afro-Cuban. See *Glosario de afronegrismos* (Havana: Imprenta "El Siglo XX," 1924), pp. 47-49.

8. The extraordinary wealth that flowed to Cuba during the "Dance of the Millions," which was a result of the high price of sugar on the international market, profoundly altered the value system of the young republic by creating a new commercial aristocracy whose life style was held up for emulation, supplanting the influence of the traditional educated elite. When the crash came in 1925, materialism was still highly valued, despite the socioeconomic dislocation. For a detailed study of the period, see Rosalie Schwartz, "The Displaced and the Disappointed: Cultural Nationalists and Black Activists in Cuba in the 1920's" (Ph.D. diss., University of California at San Diego, 1977).

9. See David W. Ames, "Negro Family Types in a Cuban Solar," *Phylon* 11 (1950): 162.

10. The events leading to the uprising in which several thousand blacks were massacred are still shrouded in mystery. In 1908, an Independent Colored Party was formed by disgruntled veterans of the Wars of Independence to seek redress for political neglect. The formation of the party was opposed by blacks who were active members of the traditional political parties. In 1910, an amendment to the electoral law made it illegal for political parties to be structured solely on the basis of race. The confrontation occurred when members of the Independent Colored Party refused to accept their illegal

status. For further details, see Rafael Fermoselle, *Política y color en Cuba: La guerrita de 1912* (Montevideo: Ediciones Géminis, 1974); and Thomas T. Orum, "The Politics of Color: The Racial Dimension of Cuban Politics during the Early Republican Years, 1900-1912" (Ph.D. diss., New York University, 1975), pp. 187-264.

11. While Guillén's unemployed black characters are frequently perceived as irresponsible, their situation was a reflection of the national economic crisis that occurred after the sugarbased economy collapsed in 1925.

12. The word, "chévere" (dandy), derives from "Má chébere," one of the praise names of Mokongo, the chief who represents military power in the Abakuá secret society. The name came to be synonymous with *ñáñigo*, members of the mutual-aid society, which was introduced in Cuba by Africans from Calabar at the beginning of the nineteenth century. Because the society placed a premium on bravery and fearlessness, it eventually became a haven for criminal elements. See Lydia Cabrera, *La sociedad secreta Abakuá narrada por viejos adeptos* (Miami: Ediciones C.R., 1970), pp. 10, 20-21, 166-68.

13. Women were explicitly excluded from membership in the Abakuá society because, according to the charter myth of the society, a woman had violated the original taboo of secrecy. Lydia Cabrera, *El monte. Igbo Finda Ewe Orisha, Vititi Nfinda (Notas sobre las religiones, la magia, las supersticiones y el folklore de los negros criollos y del pueblo de Cuba)* (Miami: Colección del Chicherekú, 1971), pp. 207-09, 277-87.

14. According to Lydia Cabrera, Afro-Cubans consider the waning moon as a symbol of diminishing strength. Thus, projects begun under the sign of a waning moon were believed to end in death. Ibid., pp. 118-21.

15. On the necessity of Latin American males to publicly demonstrate their potency, see Evelyn P. Stevens, "Machismo and Marianismo," *Society* 10 (September-October 1973): 57-63.

16. Frantz Fanon, *The Wretched*, pp. 52-54.

17. Constance Sparrow de García-Barrio, "The Black in Cuban Literature and the Poetry of Nicolás Guillén" (Ph.D. diss., University of Pennsylvania, 1975), p. 125.

18. Orlando Patterson, "Rethinking Black History," *Africa Report* 17 (November-December 1972): 29.

19. Knight, *Slave Society*, pp. 68-84, 113-36.

20. For a discussion of the factors leading to the abolition of slavery in 1886, such as British pressure on Spain to end the slave trade, the effects of a domestic and international abolitionist movement, the example of the American Civil War and the freeing of American slaves, the outbreak of Cuba's Ten Years' War and the incipient movement for independence from Spain, the invention of the steam engine, which led to the introduction of modern machines and railroads, and the increasing mechanization of the Cuban sugar industry, see Knight, *Slave Society*, pp. 137-78.

21. It has been argued that the constitutional guarantee of equality before the law is discriminatory in that only the homeless poor were likely to violate

the law against sleeping in vestibules. See Blas Roca, *Los fundamentos del socialismo en Cuba* (Havana: Editorial Páginas, 1943), p. 94.

22. See Alberto Arredondo, *El negro en Cuba* (Havana: Editorial Alfa, 1939), pp. 158-59.

23. On the predominant role of the military in protecting the sugar harvest and in crushing the fledgling labor movement, particularly under Machado and Batista, see Louis A. Pérez, Jr., *Army Politics in Cuba, 1898-1958* (Pittsburgh: University of Pittsburgh Press, 1976), pp. 58-67, 102-15.

24. According to Blas Roca, not only were blacks systematically excluded from the better-paying jobs, but political uprisings like that of 1912 usually served as a pretext for depriving them of their property. See *Los fundamentos*, pp. 75-87.

25. Coulthard, *Race and Colour*, pp. 23-26.

26. Lydia Cabrera has stated that despite the professed oaths of undying brotherly love taken by *ñáñigos*, their cult of virility often led them to compete with each other in an effort to demonstrate their superior strength, and this resulted in many violent deaths. See *Anaforuana: Ritual y símbolos de la iniciación en la sociedad secreta Abakuá* (Madrid: Ediciones R, 1975), pp. 12-13.

27. Ibid., pp. 7-8.

28. For an analysis of this aspect of the poem, see Lowery, "Selected Poems," pp. 110-11.

29. On the genesis of the one-dimensional image of blacks in Hispanic literature and its impact on Guillén's early work, see Lemuel Johnson, *The Devil*, pp. 66-81, 136-44.

30. Mervyn Alleyne, "The Linguistic Continuity of Africa in the Caribbean," *Black Academy Review* 1 (Winter 1970): 13.

31. Humberto López Morales, "La lengua de la poesía afrocubana," *Español Actual* 7 (May 10, 1967): 1-3.

32. It has been argued that, under the guise of promoting racial harmony, *mestizaje* in Latin America effectively means the loss of black identity. See Richard L. Jackson, *The Black Image in Latin American Literature* (Albuquerque: University of New Mexico Press, 1976), pp. 1-8, 91-93.

33. The prologue opens with an admission that the poems will be upsetting to many because they deal with blacks and other popular classes. After identifying the verses as "mulatto" and stating that Cuba is culturally "mestizo," it ends with the hope of hastening the day when "the definitive color" will be "Cuban color." See Guillén, *Obra poética*, 1: 113-14.

34. For a detailed account of the mixed reactions to Guillén's early poems, see Augier, *Notas*, 1: 130-42.

35. Elizabeth Sutherland, *The Youngest Revolution: A Personal Report on Cuba* (New York: Dial Press, 1969), p. 138.

Chapter 4

1. Juan René Betancourt, *El negro: Ciudadano del futuro* (Havana: Editorial O.N.R.E., 1959). My translation.

2. Aimé Césaire, *Discourse on Colonialism*, trans. Joan Pinkham (New York: Monthly Review Press, 1972), p. 21.

3. René Depestre, "Problemas de la identidad del hombre negro en las literaturas antillanas," *Casa de las Américas* 53 (March-April 1969): 20. My translation.

4. Ibid., p. 27.

5. On the combination of moral, political and economic imperatives motivating the Spanish conquest of the New World, and the institutional means used by the Spanish Crown to bring the area and its *conquistadores* under control, see Franklin W. Knight, *The Caribbean: The Genesis of a Fragmented Nationalism* (New York: Oxford University Press, 1978), pp. 23–66.

6. Stuart Hall, "Pluralism, Race and Class in Caribbean Society," in *Race and Class in Post-Colonial Society: A Study of Ethnic Group Relations in the English-Speaking Caribbean, Bolivia, Chile and Mexico*, ed. John Rex (Paris: UNESCO, 1977), pp. 172–73.

7. Lamming, *Exile*, pp. 12–36.

8. For an elaboration of the theory and its application to Latin America, see Norman Girvan, *Aspects of the Political Economy of Race in the Caribbean and the Americas: A Preliminary Interpretation* (Mona, Jamaica: Institute of Social and Economic Research, 1975), pp. 2–8, 19–22, 27–30.

9. Depestre, "Problemas," p. 21.

10. Cf. Herbert S. Klein, *Slavery in the Americas: A Comparative Study of Virginia and Cuba* (Chicago: University of Chicago Press, 1967), pp. 58–66, 73–85.

11. Despite the early legal attempts by the Spanish to minimize social contacts between the members of the various races, the fact that there were few women among the European and African groups led to interracial sexual unions and to the birth of a growing number of racially mixed persons. See Leslie B. Rout, Jr., *The African Experience in Spanish America: 1502 to the Present Day* (New York: Cambridge University Press, 1976), pp. 25–26, 71–80.

12. The racially mixed society generated a bewildering number of terms for classifying persons of mixed blood according to their degree of Europeanness. After Cuba became a major plantation society, blacks became a majority of the population, thereby causing social control to be a primary worry for Cuban landowners during the nineteenth century. Fear of slave rebellions was a constant preoccupation. In the wake of the Haitian Revolution, vigorous attempts were made to curtail the movements of the growing colored population, both slave and free, and this resulted not only in the implementation of harsher laws, but also in the massacre of thousands of blacks in 1844, in what was perceived to be a push for political autonomy. See Knight, *Slave Society*, pp. 59–100, 121–25.

13. On the biracial composition of the forces involved in the struggle for independence, see Rout, *The African Experience*, pp. 296-97, 301-02.

14. For a personal statement on the phenomenon of "internal exile" among Latin American intellectuals, see Roberto Fernández Retamar, *Ensayo de otro mundo* (Santiago, Chile: Editorial Universitaria, 1969), pp. 75-77.

15. Fanon, *The Wretched*, p. 83.

16. It was observed in 1946 that canefields occupied well over half of all cultivated land, and usually the best land. See Lowry Nelson, *Rural Cuba* (Minneapolis: University of Minnesota Press, 1950), pp. 47-59, 94-104.

17. On the role reversal between land and canefield in Guillén's poem, see Augier, *Notas*, 1: 152-53.

18. Contrary to popular belief, there existed an influential group of Cuban landowners, despite the increasing encroachment of American corporations after 1906 and the elimination of several small proprietors with the onset of the depression in 1925. All Cubans were resentful of the encroachment of the American corporation. In 1926, government regulations attempted to control foreign ownership of Cuban land. See Nelson, *Rural Cuba*, pp. 88-105.

19. See Jorge I. Domínguez, *Cuba: Order and Revolution* (Cambridge, Mass.: Harvard University Press, 1978), pp. 20-24.

20. The tendency toward monoculture in itself made for inefficient land use, since each year several acres of mill-owned land were deliberately withheld from cultivation in a country where land hunger was great. Moreover, the quota system of production, introduced in 1937 to protect the small grower from economic disaster by guaranteeing him a fixed income for a predetermined supply of cane, meant that there was no incentive for small farmers to improve the quantity and/or quality of their crops. Thus, yields were only half of what they might have been. See James O'Connor, *The Origins of Socialism in Cuba* (Ithaca, N.Y.: Cornell University Press, 1970), pp. 14-26, 59-69, 82-89.

21. On the substandard living conditions in rural Cuba, Ibid., pp. 55-59.

22. The Cuban Army of Liberation was disbanded in 1899 and a new army was subsequently formed under American supervision in order to control civil disorder, for there was no adequate police force. Treaty agreements with the United States placed on the United States the burden of defending the island against foreign aggression. The army's stake in maintaining political stability was increased under Machado (1925-1933), who, to demonstrate his ability to protect foreign lives and property (the criterion by which the viability of his government was judged by the United States) used the army not only to guard property and to restore services interrupted by strikes, but also to intimidate and assassinate labor leaders and to impose martial law. When Batista seized power by coup in 1952, he continued Machado's policy of brutally suppressing labor unrest. Even when Batista was engaged in resisting the Castro challenge, troops were assigned to protect the sugar harvest. See Louis A. Pérez, *Army Politics in Cuba, 1898-1958*, (Pittsburgh: University of Pittsburgh Press, 1976), pp. 4-67, 101-07, 114-15, 128-62.

23. On the circumstances leading to Cuba's adoption of the Platt Amendment, despite local opposition, see Luis Aguilar, *Cuba 1933: Prologue to Revolution* (Ithaca, N.Y.: Cornell University Press, 1972), pp. 12–20; Philip S. Foner, *The Spanish-Cuban-American War and the Birth of American Imperialism, 1895–1902*, 2 vols. (New York: Monthly Review Press, 1972).

24. For a discussion of the reasons for American intervention from 1906 to 1909, in 1912, and from 1917 to 1922, see Domínguez, *Cuba*, pp. 11–19.

25. In 1949, U.S. marines defaced the Martí statue in Havana's Central Park. See Ruscalleda Bercedóniz, *Nicolás Guillén*, p. 115.

26. For an analysis of the political shortcomings of early republican governments and the problems of legitimacy created by their acceptance of client status, see Domínguez, *Cuba*, pp. 11–53.

27. According to Luis Aguilar, a lack of other career opportunities meant that politics in prerevolutionary Cuba was seen as an avenue to personal success. See *Cuba 1933*, p. 33.

28. See Domínguez, *Cuba*, pp. 58–66, 99–100.

29. A standard argument in Latin American intellectual history of the twentieth century is the idea of two cultures in conflict: a spiritual Latin America threatened by a materialistic United States. The argument was first stated by José Enrique Rodó in *Ariel* in 1900, when the defeat of Spain by the United States led to a realization that America was emerging as a world power and fear of the consequences. For a recent restatement of the issue, see Roberto Fernández Retamar, "Caliban: Notes towards a Discussion of Culture in Our America," trans. David Arthur McMurray and Robert Márquez, *The Massachusetts Review* 15 (Winter-Spring 1974): 7–72.

30. An even more devastating view of the exploitative nature of tourism in tropical countries was subsequently expressed by Fanon in *The Wretched*, pp. 153–54.

31. Johnson, *The Devil*, p. 151.

32. Melon, *Realidad, poesía e ideología*, p. 46.

Chapter 5

1. The idea that social existence determines consciousness rather than that consciousness determines social existence is one of Marx's fundamental tenets. See John McMurtry, *The Structure of Marx's World-View* (Princeton, N.J.: Princeton University Press, 1978), pp. 39–45.

2. To Marx, the goal of a truly liberated existence would be achieved when all human activity was marked by the creativity and freedom from external constraints presumably enjoyed by the artist. On art as a paradigm of non-alienated labor, ibid., pp. 24–36.

3. Marx believed that man was distinguished from other animals by his capacity to create consciously the means for satisfying his material needs. Since this was considered to be a fundamental human characteristic, Marx thought that

men who lived in oppressive social conditions would experience the need to be the owners of the product of their labor and would therefore act to gain control over their working conditions. Self-realization was therefore the result of man's satisfying his innate desire for material well-being. Ibid., pp. 21–23, 29–32.

4. See Hartmut Ramm, *The Marxism of Régis Debray: Between Lenin and Guevara* (Lawrence, Kans.: The Regents Press of Kansas, 1978), p. 7.

5. According to Marxist thought, the emancipation of the workers would be achieved through the conscious action of the workers themselves and not simply through the actions of the leaders and the revolutionary vanguard. For a recent restatement of this view, see Michael Lowy, *The Marxism of Che Guevara. Philosophy, Economics, and Revolutionary Warfare*, trans. Brian Pearce (New York: Monthly Review Press, 1973), pp. 20–23.

6. Cuban workers who were members of Communist-led unions received little education in political matters, and tended to become members of those unions not for ideological reasons, but because their leaders were viewed as being "more personally honest and dedicated" than the leaders of other trade unions. Despite a history of militant struggle, Cuban workers tended to seek limited economic goals and therefore had no overall strategy for seizing state power and reshaping Cuban society for the benefit of their class. As recently as 1970, Castro lamented the absence of a working-class consciousness. See Samuel Farber, *Revolution and Reaction in Cuba, 1933–1960: A Political Sociology from Machado to Castro* (Middletown, Conn.: Wesleyan University Press, 1976), pp. 10–13, 134–35, 140–44.

7. Cold War politics as well as competition from government-supported unions helped to undermine the strength of the Communist-controlled labor unions. Increasing government intervention in the economy after 1933 also weakened the unions, whose leaders became more reliant on government support for survival. Ibid., pp. 130–40.

8. For a first-hand account of government harassment, see Roca, *Los fundamentos*, p. 94.

9. On the vacillations of the various parties over the years resulting from internal dissension, their misreading of the domestic situation, their minority status, and rigid control from Moscow, which led to their lack of participation in the major historical events of the twentieth century, see Luis Aguilar, ed., *Marxism in Latin America* (Philadelphia: Temple University Press, 1978), pp. 10–42.

10. For an account of Guatemala's political experiment between 1944 and 1954, the internal problems of the governments involved, and the CIA-backed invasion that finally overthrew the Arbenz government, see Susanne Jonas, "Guatemala: Land of Eternal Struggle," in Chilcote and Edelstein, *Latin America*, pp. 138–76.

11. The Marxist view of history is essentially linear and is believed to consist of three stages. In the initial, primitive, stage, men were considered to live in harmony with each other and with nature in a classless society, but in depressed economic and cultural conditions. The second stage, capitalism,

is believed to be an improvement on the first because man uses technology to create more goods for himself and for his fellow men. However, man's greater control over nature means the fragmentation of society into classes antagonistic to each other and the alienation of man himself by his separation from the products of his labor. The final stage, modern communism, is perceived to be an improvement on capitalism in that it would seek to extend the material and cultural abundance achieved under capitalism to all men in society rather than to privileged classes. Thus, the harmony and equality of primitive communism would prevail in an environment of prosperity. See G. A. Cohen, *Karl Marx's Theory of History: A Defence* (Princeton, N.J.: Princeton University Press, 1978), pp. 22-26.

12. Ibid., pp. 80-215.

13. On the marginality of the peasant, see Roca, *Los fundamentos*, pp. 65-74.

14. Ibid., pp. 27-32.

15. This was Castro's subsequent belief. See Ramm, *Régis Debray*, p. 18.

16. On Guevara's theory of the centrality of the countryside to revolutionary struggle, ibid., pp. 17-22.

17. Ángel Augier, "La revolución cubana," p. 54.

18. The standard view of Latin American Communist parties was that imperialism, rather than the capitalist system, was the enemy. Hence the focus on revolutionary nationalism rather than on the defeat of capitalism by socialism. See Ramm, *Régis Debray*, p. 11.

19. For a recent statement of the Marxist view of the overcoming of alienation under socialism, see Lowy, *Che Guevara*, pp. 15-17.

20. The idea of the "new man" who is totally identified with his community is a standard Marxist concept that was subsequently reformulated by Che Guevara. Ibid., pp. 25-34.

21. On the role of technology in Marx's thought, ibid., pp. 39-62.

Chapter 6

1. Ernesto Guevara, "El socialismo y el hombre en Cuba," in Ernesto Guevara et al., *El hombre nuevo* (Buenos Aires: Editorial del Noroeste, 1973), pp. 23-36.

2. The debate, which took place between 1963 and 1965, was resolved between 1966 and 1970 in favor of moral incentives. Since 1970, a combination of moral and material incentives have been implemented. For a recent summary and analysis of the various positions in the debate, see Terry Karl, "Work Incentives in Cuba," *Latin American Perspectives*, 2 (Supp. 1975): 21-41.

3. Richard R. Fagen, *The Transformation of Political Culture in Cuba* (Stanford, Calif.: Stanford University Press, 1969).

4. For an examination of the role of the intellectual in Cuba through 1971, see

Judith A. Weiss, *"Casa de las Américas"*: *An Intellectual Review of the Cuban Revolution* (Chapel Hill, N.C.: Estudios de Hispanófila, 1977).

5. Fidel Castro, *Palabras a los intelectuales* (Montevideo: Comité de Intelectuales y Artistas de apoyo a la Revolución Cubana, 1961), p. 12. For a study of the relationship between official policy and literature, see Seymour Menton, "Literature and Revolution," in his *Prose Fiction of the Cuban Revolution* (Austin, Tex.: University of Texas Press, 1975), pp. 123-56.

6. Article 38(d) of the Socialist Constitution adopted in 1976 states: "Artistic creativity is free as long as its content is not contrary to the Revolution. Forms of expression of art is free." See *Constitution of the Republic of Cuba* (New York: Center for Cuban Studies, 1976), p. 13. According to one student of the constitution, the following provisions of Article 61 make it possible for the government to override the concessions made to artistic freedom in Article 38(d): "None of the freedoms which are recognized for the citizens can be exercised contrary to what is established in the Constitution and the law, or contrary to the existence and objectives of the socialist state, or contrary to the decision of the Cuban people to build socialism and communism. Violations of this principle can be punished by law." See Leonel-Antonio de la Cuesta, "The Cuban Socialist Constitution: Its Originality and Role in Institutionalization," *Cuban Studies/Estudios Cubanos* 6 (July 1976): 19-20.

7. Nelson P. Valdés, "Revolution and Institutionalization in Cuba," *Cuban Studies /Estudios Cubanos* 6 (January and July 1976): 6-12.

8. Regarding the attempt to dispense with market mechanisms and to deemphasize the role of money, see Carmelo Mesa-Lago, "Ideological, Political, and Economic Factors in the Cuban Controversy on Material Versus Moral Incentives," *Journal of Interamerican Studies and World Affairs* 14 (February 1972): 49-111.

9. René Depestre, "Paseo por el gran zoo de Nicolás Guillén," in René Depestre, *Por la Revolución, por la poesía* (Havana: Instituto del Libro, 1969), pp. 163-64.

10. On the strategic importance of spreading the Revolution because of Cuba's isolation in the hemisphere, see C. Ian Lumsden, "The Ideology of the Revolution," in *Cuba in Revolution*, ed. Rolando E. Bonachea and Nelson P. Valdés (Garden City, N.Y.: Doubleday and Co., 1972), pp. 529-44.

11. On the problem of exporting the Revolution because of changed international circumstances, including Guevara's death and the hostility of other Latin American leaders to "revolutionary imperialism," see Ernesto F. Betancourt, "Exporting the Revolution to Latin America," in Mesa-Lago, *Revolutionary Change*, pp. 105-25.

12. Regarding the appeals to José Martí in the 1930s and 1940s by politicians seeking to legitimize their behavior, see Nita R. Manitzas, "The Setting of the Cuban Revolution," Warner Modular Publications, Module 260 (1973), pp. 15-17.

13. On exile as a means of siphoning off political discontent, see Fagen, *Political Culture*, p. 8.

14. Regarding discrimination against Afro-Cubans by other Cubans, see Benigno E. Aguirre, "Differential Migration of Cuban Social Races: A Review and Interpretation of the Problem," *Latin American Research Review*, 11 (Spring 1976): 114.

15. Ibid., pp. 112-16.

16. Cf. Jackson, *The Black Image*, pp. 15-17; Lloyd King, "Nicolás Guillén and Afrocubanismo," in *A Celebration of Black and African Writing*, ed. Bruce King and Kolawole Ogungbesan (Zaria, Nigeria: Ahmadu Bello University Press and Oxford University Press, 1975), pp. 42-44; Barry Reckord, *Does Fidel Eat More Than Your Father?: Conversations in Cuba* (New York: Praeger Publishers, 1971), pp. 124-40; Andrew Salkey, *Havana Journal* (Middlesex: Penguin Books, 1971), pp. 21-22, 157-58.

17. Fernández Retamar, *Ensayo*, p. 157.

18. Robert Márquez, "Introduction," *Man-Making Words*, p. xvi.

19. Constance Sparrow de García-Barrio, "The Image of the Black Man in the Poetry of Nicolás Guillén," in DeCosta, *Blacks in Hispanic Literature*, p. 110.

20. Fidel Castro made several statements to this effect. In a recent interview, Guillén expressed a similar view. See Keith Ellis, "Conversation with Nicolás Guillén," *Jamaica Journal* 7 (March-June 1973): 78-79. For a dissenting view, see Betancourt, *El negro*, pp. 161-70.

21. Carlos More, "Le peuple noir a-t-il sa place dans la révolution cubaine?," *Présence Africaine* 52 (1964): 177-230.

22. Rout, *The African Experience*, p. 308.

23. *El tiro al blanco* is literally "the shot on the white (patch)," i.e., "the target"; *el tiro al negro* is literally "shooting the black man."

24. Regarding various patterns of instant mobility, see Fagen, *Political Culture*, p. 119, pp. 145-47.

25. See Carmelo Mesa-Lago, "The Revolutionary Offensive," *Trans-action* 6 (April 1969): 22-29, 62.

26. Fagen, *Political Culture*, pp. 12-31.

27. On Cuban-American relations, see Cole Blasier, "The Elimination of United States Influence," in Mesa-Lago, *Revolutionary Change*, pp. 43-80. On Cuban relations with the Soviet Union up to 1970, see Edward González, "Relationship with the Soviet Union," in Mesa-Lago, *Revolutionary Change*, pp. 81-104. For relations with the Soviet Union since 1970, see Mesa-Lago, *Cuba in the 1970's: Pragmatism and Institutionalization* (Albuquerque: University of New Mexico Press, 1978), pp. 10-25.

28. Lourdes Casal, "Literature and Society," in Mesa-Lago, *Revolutionary Change*, p. 449. Cf. G. R. Coulthard, "The Situation of the Writer in Contemporary Cuba," *Caribbean Studies* 7 (April 1967): 30.

29. Keith Ellis, "Cuban Literature and the Revolution," *The Canadian Forum* 48 (January 1969): 224.

Conclusion

1. See Jean Franco *The Modern Culture of Latin America: Society and the Artist* (Middlesex: Penguin Books, 1970), pp. 11-12, 311.

2. For further details, see M. A. Pérez-Medina, "The Situation of the Negro in Cuba," in *Negro Anthology, 1931-1933*, ed. Nancy Cunard (New York: Negro Universities Press, 1969), pp. 480-81.

3. Cf. José Luis Varela, *Ensayos de poesía indígena en Cuba* (Madrid: Ediciones Cultura Hispánica, 1951), pp. 77-88.

4. See Schwartz, "The Displaced."

5. See Domínguez, *Cuba*, pp. 38-44.

6. In a recent interview, Guillén made a statement to this effect. See Ellis, "Conversation," p. 78.

SELECTED
BIBLIOGRAPHY

Works by Guillén

Obra poética, 1920-1972. 2 vols. Havana: Instituto Cubano del Libro, 1974.
Antología mayor: El son entero y otros poemas. Havana: UNEAC, 1964.
Antología mayor. Mexico: Editorial Diógenes, 1972.
Cantos para soldados y sones para turistas. Mexico: Editorial Masas, 1937.
El corazón con que vivo. Havana: UNEAC, 1975.
El diario que a diario. Havana: UNEAC, 1972.
El gran zoo. Buenos Aires: Editorial Quetzal, 1967.
Motivos de son. Havana: Impr. Rambla, Bouza, 1930.
La paloma de vuelo popular. Elegías. Buenos Aires: Editorial Losada, 1958.
Poemas de amor. Havana: Ediciones La Tertulia, 1964.
Por qué imperialismo: Poema. Bogotá: Ediciones Calarca, 1976.
Prosa de prisa; crónicas. Santa Clara, Cuba: Universidad Central de Las Villas, 1962.
Prosa de prisa; crónicas. Buenos Aires: Editorial Hernández, 1968.
Prosa de prisa, 1929-1972. Edited by Ángel Augier. 2 vols. Havana: Editorial Arte y Literatura, 1975.
La rueda dentada. Havana: UNEAC, 1972.
El son entero, cantos para soldados y sones para turistas. Buenos Aires: Editorial Losada, 1952.
El son entero, suma poética, 1929-1946. Buenos Aires: Editorial Pleamar, 1947.
Sóngoro cosongo; Motivos de son; West Indies, Ltd.; España, poema en cuatro angustias y una esperanza. Buenos Aires: Editorial Losada, 1952.
Sóngoro cosongo, poemas mulatos. Havana: Úcar García, 1931.
Sóngoro cosongo y otros poemas. Havana: La Verónica, 1942.
Summa poética. Edited by Luis Iñigo Madrigal. Madrid: Ediciones Cátedra, 1976.
Tengo. Santa Clara, Cuba: Universidad Central de Las Villas, 1964.
Tengo. Montevideo: Editorial El Siglo Ilustrado, 1967.
West Indies, Ltd., poemas. Havana: Úcar García, 1934.

Anthologies and Translations

Carr, Richard J. *Tengo*. Detroit: Broadside Press, 1974.

Couffon, Claude. *Nicolás Guillén*. Paris: Editions Pierre Seghers, 1964.

Márquez, Robert, and McMurray, David Arthur. *Man-Making Words*. Amherst: University of Massachusetts Press, 1972.

Márquez, Robert. *¡Patria o Muerte! The Great Zoo and Other Poems by Nicolás Guillén*. New York: Monthly Review Press, 1972.

Rodríguez Monegal, Emir, ed. *The Borzoi Anthology of Latin American Literature*. 2 vols. New York: Alfred A. Knopf, 1977.

Ruiz del Vizo, Hortensia, ed. *Black Poetry of the Americas (A Bilingual Anthology)*. Miami: Ediciones Universal, 1972.

Secondary Sources

Books

Aguilar, Luis E. *Cuba 1933: Prologue to Revolution*. Ithaca, N.Y.: Cornell University Press, 1972.

———, ed. *Marxism in Latin America*. Philadelphia: Temple University Press, 1978.

Alderete Ramírez, Ada Nilda. *El sonido y el ritmo en la poesía de Nicolás Guillén*. Argentina: La Banda, 1969.

Arredondo, Alberto. *El negro en Cuba*. Havana: Editorial Alfa, 1939.

Augier, Ángel. *Nicolás Guillén: Notas para un estudio biográfico-crítico*. 2 vols. Havana: Universidad Central de Las Villas, 1964.

Barrett, Leonard E. *Soul Force*. New York: Doubleday and Co., 1974.

Bascom, William. *Shango in the New World*. Austin: University of Texas Press, 1972.

Bastide, Roger. *African Civilisations in the New World*. Translated by Peter Green. London: C. Hurst and Co., 1971.

Beckford, George L. *Persistent Poverty: Underdevelopment in Plantation Economies of the Third World*. New York: Oxford University Press, 1972.

Betancourt, Juan René. *El negro: Ciudadano del futuro*. Havana: Editorial O.N.R.E., 1959.

Bonachea, Rolando E., and Valdés, Nelson P., eds. *Cuba in Revolution*. Garden City, N.Y.: Doubleday and Co., 1972.

Brotherston, Gordon. *Latin American Poetry: Origins and Presence*. Cambridge: At the University Press, 1975.

Bruns, Gerald L. *Modern Poetry and the Idea of Language: A Critical and Historical Study*. New Haven, Conn.: Yale University Press, 1974.

Cabrera, Lydia. *Anaforuana. Ritual y símbolos de la iniciación en la sociedad secreta Abakuá*. Madrid: Ediciones R, 1975.

———. *El monte. Igbo Finda Ewe Orisha, Vititi Nfinda (Notas sobre las religiones, la magia, las supersticiones y el folklore de los negros criollos y del pueblo de Cuba)*. Miami: Colección del Chicherekú, 1971.

———. *La sociedad secreta Abakuá narrada por viejos adeptos*. Miami: Ediciones C.R., 1970.

Cardenal, Ernesto. *In Cuba*. Translated by Donald D. Walsh. New York: New Directions, 1974.

Carpentier, Alejo. *La música en Cuba*. Mexico: Fondo de Cultura Económica, 1972.

Carrera Andrade, Jorge. *Reflections on Spanish-American Poetry*. Translated by Don C. Bliss and Gabriela de C. Bliss. Albany, N.Y.: State University of New York Press, 1973.

Cartey, Wilfred G. *Black Images*. New York: Teacher's College Press, 1970.

Castro, Fidel. *Palabras a los intelectuales*. Montevideo: Comité de Intelectuales y Artistas de apoyo a la Revolución Cubana, 1961.

Césaire, Aimé. *Discourse on Colonialism*. Translated by Joan Pinkham. New York: Monthly Review Press, 1972.

Chilcote, Ronald H., and Edelstein, Joel C., eds. *Latin America: The Struggle with Dependency and Beyond*. Cambridge, Mass.: Schenkman Publishing Co., 1974.

Clytus, John. *Black Man in Red Cuba*. Coral Gables, Fla.: University of Miami Press, 1970.

Cobb, Martha. *Harlem, Haiti, and Havana. A Comparative Critical Study of Langston Hughes, Jacques Roumain, and Nicolás Guillén*. Washington, D.C.: Three Continents Press, 1979.

Cohen, G. A. *Karl Marx's Theory of History: A Defence*. Princeton, N.J.: Princeton University Press, 1978.

Constitution of the Republic of Cuba. New York: Center for Cuban Studies, 1976.

Coulthard, G. R. *Race and Colour in Caribbean Literature*. London: Oxford University Press, 1962.

Coward, Rosalind, and Ellis, John. *Language and Materialism. Developments in Semiology and the Theory of the Subject*. London: Routledge and Kegan Paul, 1977.

Crahan, Margaret E., and Knight, Franklin W., eds. *Africa and the Caribbean: The Legacies of a Link*. Baltimore: The Johns Hopkins University Press, 1979.

Cunard, Nancy, ed. *Negro Anthology, 1931-1933*. New York: Negro Universities Press, 1969.

Dathorne, O. R. *The Black Mind: A History of African Literature*. Minneapolis: University of Minnesota Press, 1974.

DeCosta, Miriam, ed. *Blacks in Hispanic Literature: Critical Essays*. Port Washington, N.Y.: Kennikat Press, 1977.

Depestre, René. *Por la Revolución, por la poesía*. Havana: Instituto del Libro, 1969.

Domínguez, Jorge I. *Cuba: Order and Revolution*. Cambridge, Mass.: Harvard University Press, 1978.

Ehrmann, Jacques, ed. *Literature and Revolution*. Boston: Beacon Press, 1970.

Fagen, Richard R. *The Transformation of Political Culture in Cuba*. Stanford, Calif.: Stanford University Press, 1969.

Fanon, Frantz. *Black Skin, White Masks*. Translated by Charles Lam Markmann. New York: Grove Press, 1967.

———. *The Wretched of the Earth*. Translated by Constance Farrington. New York: Grove Press, 1968.

Farber, Samuel. *Revolution and Reaction in Cuba, 1933-1960: A Political Sociology from Machado to Castro*. Middletown, Conn.: Wesleyan University Press, 1976.

Fermoselle, Rafael. *Política y color en Cuba: La guerrita de 1912*. Montevideo: Ediciones Géminis, 1974.

Fernández de Castro, José Antonio. *Tema negro en las letras de Cuba (1608-1935)*. Havana: Ediciones Mirador, 1943.

Fernández Retamar, Roberto. *Ensayo de otro mundo*. Santiago, Chile: Editorial Universitaria, 1969.

———. *El son de vuelo popular*. Havana: Instituto Cubano del Libro, 1972.

Fernández de la Vega, Oscar, and Pamies, Alberto N., eds. *Iniciación a la poesía afro-americana*. Miami: Ediciones Universal, 1973.

Finnegan, Ruth. *Oral Literature in Africa*. London: Oxford University Press, 1970.

Foner, Philip S. *The Spanish-Cuban-American War and the Birth of American Imperialism, 1895-1902*. 2 vols. New York: Monthly Review Press, 1972.

Franco, Jean. *The Modern Culture of Latin America: Society and the Artist*. Middlesex: Penguin Books, 1970.

Girvan, Norman. *Aspects of the Political Economy of Race in the Caribbean and the Americas: A Preliminary Interpretation*. Mona, Jamaica: Institute of Social and Economic Research, 1975.

Grundy, Kenneth W. *Guerrilla Struggle in Africa: An Analysis and Preview*. New York: Grossman Publishers, 1971.

Guevara, Ernesto, et al. *El hombre nuevo*. Buenos Aires: Editorial del Noroeste, 1973.

Hoetink, H. *Caribbean Race Relations: A Study of Two Variants*. Translated by Eva M. Hooykaas. London: Oxford University Press, 1971.

——. *Slavery and Race Relations in the Americas: Comparative Notes on Their Nature and Nexus*. New York: Harper and Row, 1973.

Horowitz, Michael M., ed. *Peoples and Cultures of the Caribbean*. Garden City, N.Y.: The Natural History Press, 1971.

Jackson, Richard L. *The Black Image in Latin American Literature*. Albuquerque: University of New Mexico Press, 1976.

——. *Black Writers in Latin America*. Albuquerque: University of New Mexico Press, 1979.

Jahn, Janheinz. *Muntu: An Outline of the New African Culture*. Translated by Marjorie Grene. New York: Grove Press, 1961.

Johnson, Lemuel A. *The Devil, the Gargoyle, and the Buffoon: The Negro as Metaphor in Western Literature*. Port Washington, N.Y.: Kennikat Press, 1971.

Klein, Herbert S. *Slavery in the Americas: A Comparative Study of Virginia and Cuba*. Chicago: University of Chicago Press, 1967.

Knight, Franklin W. *The African Dimension in Latin American Societies*. New York: Macmillan Publishing Co., 1974.

——. *The Caribbean: The Genesis of a Fragmented Nationalism*. New York: Oxford University Press, 1978.

——. *Slave Society in Cuba during the Nineteenth Century*. Madison: University of Wisconsin Press, 1970.

Lamming, George. *The Pleasures of Exile*. London: Michael Joseph, 1960.

López Morales, Humberto. *Estudios sobre el español de Cuba*. New York: Las Américas Publishing Co., 1971.

Lowy, Michael. *The Marxism of Che Guevara. Philosophy, Economics, and Revolutionary Warfare*. Translated by Brian Pearce. New York: Monthly Review Press, 1973.

McMurtry, John. *The Structure of Marx's World-View*. Princeton, N.J.: Princeton University Press, 1978.

Mansour, Mónica. *La poesía negrista*. Mexico: Ediciones Era, 1973.

Marinello, Juan. *Poética; ensayos en entusiasmo*. Madrid: Editorial Espasa-Calpe, 1933.

Martínez Estrada, Ezequiel. *La poesía afrocubana de Nicolás Guillén*. Montevideo: Editorial Arca, 1966.

Mbiti, John S. *African Religions and Philosophy*. New York: Frederick A. Praeger, 1969.

Melon, Alfred. *Realidad, poesía e ideología*. Havana: Ediciones Unión, 1973.

Menton, Seymour. *Prose Fiction of the Cuban Revolution*. Austin: University of Texas Press, 1975.

Mesa-Lago, Carmelo. *Cuba in the 1970's: Pragmatism and Institutionalization*. Albuquerque: University of New Mexico Press, 1978.

——, ed. *Revolutionary Change in Cuba*. Pittsburgh: University of Pittsburgh Press, 1971.

Mintz, Sidney W., ed. *Slavery, Colonialism, and Racism*. New York: W. W. Norton and Co., 1974.

Mintz, Sidney W., and Price, Richard. *An Anthropological Approach to the Afro-American Past: A Caribbean Perspective*. Philadelphia: Institute for the Study of Human Issues, 1976.

Morejón, Nancy, ed. *Recopilación de textos sobre Nicolás Guillén*. Havana: Casa de las Américas, 1974.

Nelson, Lowry. *Rural Cuba*. Minneapolis: University of Minnesota Press, 1950.

O'Connor, James. *The Origins of Socialism in Cuba*. Ithaca, N.Y.: Cornell University Press, 1970.

Ojo, G. J. Afolabi. *Yoruba Culture: A Geographical Analysis*. London: London University Press, 1966.

Ortiz, Fernando. *Glosario de afro-negrismos*. Havana: Imprenta "El Siglo XX," 1924.

——. *Hampa afro-cubana: Los negros brujos (apuntes para un estudio de etnología criminal)*. Madrid: Editorial América, 1917.

Pereda Valdés, Ildefonso. *Lo negro y lo mulato en la poesía cubana*. Montevideo: Ediciones Ciudadela, 1970.

Pérez, Louis A., Jr. *Army Politics in Cuba, 1898-1958*. Pittsburgh: University of Pittsburgh Press, 1976.

Ramm, Hartmut. *The Marxism of Régis Debray: Between Lenin and Guevara*. Lawrence, Kans.: The Regents Press of Kansas, 1978.

Reckord, Barry. *Does Fidel Eat More Than Your Father?: Conversations in Cuba*. New York: Praeger Publishers, 1971.

Rex, John, et al. *Race and Class in Post-Colonial Society: A Study of Ethnic Group Relations in the English-speaking Caribbean, Bolivia, Chile and Mexico*. Paris: UNESCO, 1977.

Roberts, John Storm. *Black Music of Two Worlds*. New York: William Morrow and Co., 1974.

Roca, Blas. *Los fundamentos del socialismo en Cuba*. Havana: Editorial Páginas, 1943.

Rodney, Walter. *West Africa and the Atlantic Slave-Trade*. Nairobi: East African Publishing House, 1969.

Rodríguez-Embil, Luis. *La poesía negra en Cuba*. Santiago, Chile: Universidad de Chile, 1939.

Rout, Leslie B., Jr. *The African Experience in Spanish America: 1502 to the Present Day*. New York: Cambridge University Press, 1976.

Ruscalleda Bercedóniz, Jorge María. *La poesía de Nicolás Guillén (cuatro elementos sustanciales)*. Río Piedras, Puerto Rico: Editorial Universitaria, 1975.

Salkey, Andrew. *Havana Journal*. Middlesex: Penguin Books, 1971.

Sardinha, Dennis. *The Poetry of Nicolás Guillén: An Introduction*. London: New Beacon Books, 1976.

Stabb, Martin. *In Quest of Identity*. Chapel Hill: University of North Carolina Press, 1967.

Stimson, Frederick S. *The New Schools of Spanish American Poetry*. Chapel Hill, N.C.: Estudios de Hispanófila, 1970.

Sutherland, Elizabeth. *The Youngest Revolution: A Personal Report on Cuba.* New York: Dial Press, 1969.
Thomson, George. *Marxism and Poetry.* London: Lawrence and Wishart, 1946.
Torres-Ríoseco, Arturo. *The Epic of Latin American Literature.* New York: Oxford University Press, 1942.
Tous, Adriana. *La poesía de Nicolás Guillén.* Madrid: Ediciones Cultura Hispánica, 1971.
Valdés-Cruz, Rosa E. *La poesía negroide en América.* New York: Las Américas Publishing Co., 1970.
Varela, José Luis. *Ensayos de poesía indígena en Cuba.* Madrid: Ediciones Cultura Hispánica, 1951.
Vitier, Cintio. *Lo cubano en la poesía.* Havana: Instituto del Libro, 1970.
Weiss, Judith. *"Casa de las Américas": An Intellectual Review in the Cuban Revolution.* Chapel Hill, N.C.: Estudios de Hispanófila, 1977.
Williams, Eric. *The Negro in the Caribbean.* New York: Negro Universities Press, 1969.

Unpublished Sources

Boyd, Antonio Olliz. "The Concept of Black Esthetics As Seen in Selected Works of Three Latin American Writers: Machado de Assis, Nicolás Guillén and Adalberto Ortiz." Ph.D. dissertation, Stanford University, 1974.
García-Barrio, Constance Sparrow de. "The Black in Cuban Literature and the Poetry of Nicolás Guillén." Ph.D. dissertation, University of Pennsylvania, 1975.
Hollingsworth, Charles. "The Development of Literary Theory in Cuba, 1958-68." Ph.D. dissertation, University of California at Berkeley, 1972.
Lowery, Dellita Martin. "Selected Poems of Nicolás Guillén and Langston Hughes: Their Use of Afro-Western Folk Music Genres." Ph.D. dissertation, Ohio State University, 1975.
Orum, Thomas T. "The Politics of Color: The Racial Dimension of Cuban Politics during the Early Republican Years, 1900-1912." Ph.D. dissertation, New York University, 1975.
Schwartz, Rosalie. "The Displaced and the Disappointed: Cultural Nationalists and Black Activists in Cuba in the 1920's." Ph.D. dissertation, University of California at San Diego, 1977.
Yai, Olabiyi. "Influence yoruba dans la poésie cubaine:Nicolás Guillén et la tradition poétique yoruba." Seminar Paper, Dept. of Modern European Languages, University of Ife, Nigeria, 1974-75.

Articles

Aguirre, Benigno E. "Differential Migration of Cuban Social Races: A Review and Interpretation of the Problem." *Latin American Research Review* 11 (Spring 1976): 103-24.
Aguirre, Mirta. "Maestro de poesía." In *Recopilación de textos sobre Nicolás Guillén,* edited by Nancy Morejón. Havana: Casa de las Américas, 1974.
Allen, Martha E. "Nicolás Guillén, poeta del pueblo." *Revista Iberoamericana* 15 (February-July 1949): 29-43.

Alleyne, Mervyn. "The Linguistic Continuity of Africa in the Caribbean." *Black Academy Review* 1 (Winter 1970): 3-16.

Ames, David W. "Negro Family Types in a Cuban Solar." *Phylon* 11 (1950): 159-63.

Arrom, José Juan. "La poesía afrocubana." In *Estudios de Literatura Hispanoamericana*. Havana: Úcar García, 1950.

Augier, Ángel. "Alusiones africanas en la poesía de Nicolás Guillén." *Unión* 6 (December 1968): 143-51.

———. "The Cuban Poetry of Nicolás Guillén." Translated by Joseph M. Bernstein. *Phylon* 12 (1951): 29-36.

———. "La poesía cubana y revolucionaria de Nicolás Guillén." *Cuba Internacional* 4 (June 1972): 9-23.

———. "La revolución cubana en la poesía de Nicolás Guillén." *Plural* 59 (August 1976): 47-61.

Ballagas, Emilio. "El mensaje inédito." In *Recopilación de textos sobre Nicolás Guillén*, edited by Nancy Morejón. Havana: Casa de las Américas, 1974.

Bangou, Henry. "La influencia de Africa en las literaturas antillanas." *Casa de las Américas* 56 (September-October 1969): 126-31.

Bascom, William R. "The Focus of Cuban Santería." In *Peoples and Cultures of the Caribbean*, edited by Michael M. Horowitz. Garden City, N.Y.: The Natural History Press, 1971.

———. "Yoruba Acculturation in Cuba. *Les Afro-Américains, (Mémoires de l'Institut Français d'Afrique Noire)*, Dakar 27 (1953), 163-67.

———. "The Yoruba in Cuba." *Nigeria* (Lagos) 37 (1951): 14-20.

Bedriñana, Francisco C. "La luna en la poesía negra." *Revista Bimestre Cubana* 38 (1936): 12-16.

Betancourt, Ernesto F. "Exporting the Revolution to Latin America." In *Revolutionary Change in Cuba*, edited by Carmelo Mesa-Lago. Pittsburgh: University of Pittsburgh Press, 1971.

Blasier, Cole. "The Elimination of United States Influence." In *Revolutionary Change in Cuba*, edited by Carmelo Mesa-Lago. Pittsburgh: University of Pittsburgh Press, 1971.

Boj, Silverio. "La poesía negra en Indoamérica." *Sustancia* (1939-40): 591-608.

Boulware, Kay. "Woman and Nature in *Negrismo*." *Studies in Afro-Hispanic Literature* 1 (1977): 16-25.

Boyd, Antonio Olliz. "The Concept of Black Awareness as a Thematic Approach in Latin American Literature." In *Blacks in Hispanic Literature: Critical Essays*, edited by Miriam DeCosta. Port Washington, N.Y.: Kennikat Press, 1977.

Brathwaite, Edward Kamau. "The African Presence in Caribbean Literature." In *Slavery, Colonialism, and Racism*, edited by Sidney W. Mintz. New York: W. W. Norton and Co., 1974.

Bray, Donald W., and Harding, Timothy F. "Cuba." In *Latin America: The Struggle with Dependency and Beyond*, edited by Ronald H. Chilcote and Joel C. Edelstein. Cambridge, Mass.: Schenkman Publishing Co., 1974.

Bryan, Patrick. "The Blacks of Latin America." *Caribbean Quarterly* 17 (September-December 1971): 45-52.

Bueno, Salvador. *"La canción del bongó*: Sobre la cultura mulata de Cuba." *Cuadernos Americanos* 206 (May-June 1976): 89-106.

———. "Raza, color y literatura antillana." *Casa de las Américas* 36-37 (May-August 1966): 186-89.

Campaña, Antonio. "Nicolás Guillén, sones y angustia." *Atenea* 257-258 (November-December 1946): 444-58.

Carrera Andrade, Jorge. "Nicolás Guillén, poeta del hombre común y mensajero del trópico." *Revista de las Indias* (Colombia) 28 (June 1946): 467-71.

Cartey, Wilfred G. "Como surge Nicolás Guillén en las Antillas." *Universidad de Antioquia* (Colombia) 34 (1958): 257-74.

Casal, Lourdes. "Literature and Society." In *Revolutionary Change in Cuba*, edited by Carmelo Mesa-Lago. Pittsburgh: University of Pittsburgh Press, 1971.

Cobb, Martha K. "Africa in Latin America: Customs, Culture and Literature." *Black World* 21 (August 1972): 4-19.

——. "Concepts of Blackness in the Poetry of Nicolás Guillén, Jacques Roumain, and Langston Hughes." *CLA Journal* 18 (December 1974): 262-72.

Coleman, Ben. "Black Themes in the Literature of the Caribbean." *The Rican: A Journal of Contemporary Puerto Rican Thought* 3 (Spring 1973): 48-54.

Cometta Manzoni, Aída. "Trayectoria del negro en la poesía de América." *Nosotros* 11 (September-October 1939): 196-212.

Coulthard, G. R. "'Africa' in West Indian Poetry." *Caribbean Quarterly* 4 (January 1955): 5-13.

——. "Antecedentes de la negritud en la literatura hispanoamericana." *Mundo Nuevo* 11 (May 1967): 73-77.

——. "Cuban Literature and Politics." *Caribbean Monthly Bulletin* 6 (March 1969): 5-8.

——. "The Emergence of Afro-Cuban Poetry." *Caribbean Quarterly* 2 (1953): 14-17.

——. "Nicolás Guillén and West Indian Negritude." *Caribbean Quarterly* 16 (March 1970): 52-57.

——. "The Situation of the Writer in Contemporary Cuba." *Caribbean Studies* 7 (April 1967): 23-35.

——. "Two Revolutionary Literatures." *Jamaica Journal* 8 (Summer 1974): 10-12.

Cuesta, Leonel-Antonio de la. "The Cuban Socialist Constitution: Its Originality and Role in Institutionalization." *Cuban Studies/Estudios Cubanos* 6 (July 1976): 15-30.

Davis, Paul A. "The Black Man and the Caribbean as seen by Nicolás Guillén and Luis Palés Matos." *Caribbean Quarterly* 25 (March-June 1979): 72-79.

DeCosta, Miriam. "Nicolás Guillén and His Poetry for Afro-Americans." *Black World* 22 (September 1973): 12-16.

——. "Social Lyricism and the Caribbean Poet/Rebel." *CLA Journal* 15 (June 1972): 441-51.

Depestre, René. "Los fundamentos socioculturales de nuestra identidad." *Casa de las Américas* 58 (January-February 1970): 26-34.

——. "Lettre de Cuba . . ." *Présence Africaine* 56 (1965): 105-42.

——. "Mis años luz en Cuba." *Casa de las Américas,* 51-52 (November 1968-February 1969): 17-21.

——. "Problemas de la identidad del hombre negro en las literaturas antillanas." *Casa de las Américas* 53 (March-April 1969): 19-28.

Domínguez, Ivo. "En torno a la poesía afro-hispanoamericana." *Cuadernos Hispanoamericanos* 319 (January 1977): 125-31.

Ellis, Keith. "Conversation with Nicolás Guillen." *Jamaica Journal* 7 (March-June 1973): 77-79.

——. "Cuban Literature and the Revolution." *The Canadian Forum* 48 (January 1969): 224-26.

——. "Literary Americanism and the Recent Poetry of Nicolás Guillén." *University of Toronto Quarterly* 45 (Fall 1975): 1-18.

——. "Nicolás Guillén at Seventy." *Caribbean Quarterly* 19 (March 1973): 87-94.

Fernández Retamar, Roberto. "Algunas nociones sobre la cultura en la Cuba Revolucionaria." *Hispamérica* 7 (April 1978): 43-52.

——. "Caliban: Notes towards a Discussion of Culture in Our America," translated by David Arthur McMurray and Robert Márquez. *Massachusetts Review* 15 (Winter-Spring 1974): 7-72.

Figueira, Gastón. "Dos poetas iberoamericanos de nuestro tiempo." *Revista Iberoamericana* 19 (November 1945): 107-17.

Fitz, Earl E. "The Black Poetry of Nicolás Guillén and Jorge de Lima: A Comparative Study." *Inti* 4 (Autumn 1976): 76-84.

Florit, Eugenio. "Presencia de Cuba: Nicolás Guillén, poeta entero." *Revista de América* (Bogotá) 13 (February 1948): 234-48.

Font, María Teresa. "Tres manifestaciones de especialismo poético: Federico García Lorca, Nicolás Guillén y Jorge Luis Borges." *Revista Iberoamericana* 36 (October-December 1970): 601-12.

Franco, Jean. "Before and After: Contexts of Cuban Writing." *Cambridge Review* 91 (February 1970): 104-7.

Fyfe, Christopher. "The Dynamics of African Dispersal: The Transatlantic Slave Trade." In *The African Diaspora: Interpretive Essays,* edited by Martin L. Kilson and Robert I. Rotberg. Cambridge, Mass.: Harvard University Press, 1976.

García-Barrio, Constance Sparrow de. "The Image of the Black Man in the Poetry of Nicolás Guillén." In *Blacks in Hispanic Literature,* edited by Miriam DeCosta. Port Washington, N.Y.: Kennikat Press, 1977.

González, Edward. "Relationship with the Soviet Union." In *Revolutionary Change in Cuba,* edited by Carmelo Mesa-Lago. Pittsburgh: University of Pittsburgh Press, 1971.

Graf, Henning. "África en América." *Humanitas* 15 (1974): 353-96.

Granda, Germán de. "Materials for the Socio-historical Study of the Afro-American Linguistic Elements in Spanish-Speaking Areas." *Caribbean Studies* 13 (April 1973): 110-30.

Hall, Stuart. "Pluralism, Race and Class in Caribbean Society." In *Race and Class in Post-Colonial Society: A Study of Ethnic Group Relations in the English-speaking Caribbean, Bolivia, Chile and Mexico,* edited by John Rex. Paris: UNESCO, 1977.

Harth, Dorothy Feldman. "La poesía afrocubana, sus raíces e influencias." In *Miscelánea de estudios dedicados a Fernando Ortiz.* Vol. III, pp. 789-827. Havana: Úcar García, 1956.

Hays, H. R. "Nicolás Guillén y la poesía afrocubana." In *Recopilación de textos sobre Nicolás Guillén,* edited by Nancy Morejón. Havana: Casa de las Américas, 1974.

Hernández Novás, Raúl. "La más reciente poesía de Nicolás Guillén." *Casa de las Américas* 75 (November-December 1972): 159-62.

Iñigo Madrigal, Luis. "Las elegías de Nicolás Guillén: *Elegía a Emmett Till.*" *Cuadernos de Filología* (Valparaíso, Chile) 1 (1969): 47-58.

Irish, George. "The Revolutionary Focus of Guillén's Journalism." *Caribbean Quarterly* 22 (December 1976): 68-78.

Jackson, Richard L. "Black Phobia and the White Aesthetic in Spanish American Literature." *Hispania* 58 (September 1975): 467-80.

——. *"Mestizaje* vs. Black Identity: The Color Crisis in Latin America." *Black World* 24 (July 1975): 4-21.

Jahn, Janheinz. "Poetry in Rumba Rhythms." In *Introduction to African Literature: An Anthology of Critical Writing from "Black Orpheus,"* edited by Ulli Beier. Evanston, Ill.: Northwestern University Press, 1967.

Jimenes Grullón, Juan Isidro. "Nicolás Guillén." In *Seis poetas cubanos; ensayos apologéticos.* Havana: Editorial Cromos, 1954.

Johnson, Harvey L. "Nicolás Guillén's Portraits of Blacks in Cuban Society." In *Homage to Irving A. Leonard: Essays in Hispanic Art, History and Literature,* edited by Raquel Chang-Rodríguez and Donald A. Yates. New York: Editorial Mensaje, 1977.

Jonas, Susanne. "Guatemala: Land of Eternal Struggle." In *Latin America: The Struggle with Dependency and Beyond,* edited by Ronald H. Chilcote and Joel C. Edelstein. Cambridge, Mass.: Schenkman Publishing Co., 1974.

Karl, Terry. "Work Incentives in Cuba." *Latin American Perspectives* 2 (Supplement 1975): 21-41.

King, Lloyd. "Mr. Black in Cuba." *African Studies Association of the West Indies Bulletin* 5 (1972): 21-26.

——. "Nicolás Guillén and Afrocubanismo." In *A Celebration of Black and African Writing,* edited by Bruce King and Kolawole Ogungbesan. Zaria, Nigeria: Ahmadu Bello University Press and Oxford University Press, 1975.

Knight, Franklin W. "Poet of the People." *Review* (Spring 1973): 67-69.

Lamar Schweyer, Alberto. "La musa mulata." In *Recopilación de textos sobre Nicolás Guillén,* edited by Nancy Morejón. Havana: Casa de las Américas, 1974.

Lamming, George. "Actitudes de la literatura antillana con respecto a Africa." *Casa de las Américas* 56 (September-October 1969): 120-25.

López Morales, Humberto. "Elementos africanos en el español de Cuba." *Boletín de Filología Española* 6 (July-December 1966): 27-43.

——. "La lengua de la poesía afrocubana." *Español Actual* 7 (May 10, 1967): 1-3.

Lumsden, C. Ian. "The Ideology of the Revolution." In *Cuba in Revolution,* edited by Rolando E. Bonachea and Nelson P. Valdés. Garden City, New York: Doubleday and Co., 1972.

McMurray, David Arthur. "Dos negros en el Nuevo Mundo: Notas sobre el 'Americanismo' de Langston Hughes y la cubanía de Nicolás Guillén." *Casa de las Américas* 82 (January-February 1974): 122-28.

Manitzas, Nita R. "The Setting of the Cuban Revolution." Warner Modular Publications, Module 260 (1973).

Mansour, Mónica. "Circunstancia e imágenes de la poesía negrista." *Revista de la Universidad de México* 25 (October 1970): 25-32.

Marinello, Juan. "Hazaña y triunfo americanos de Nicolás Guillén." In *Recopilación de textos sobre Nicolás Guillén,* edited by Nancy Morejón. Havana: Casa de las Américas, 1974.

——. "Negrismo y mulatismo." In *Órbita de Juan Marinello,* edited by Ángel Augier. Havana: Instituto del Libro, 1968.

Márquez, Roberto. "De rosa armado y de acero: La obra de Nicolás Guillén." *Sin Nombre* 4 (October-December 1973): 23-32.

——. "Introducción a Guillén."*Casa de las Américas* 65-66 (March-June 1971): 136-42.

——. "Zombi to Synthesis: Notes on the Negro in Spanish American Literature." *Jamaica Journal* 11 (August 1977): 22-31.

Matheus, John F. "African Footprints in Hispanic-American Literature." *Journal of Negro History* 23 (July 1938): 265-89.

Megenney, William W. "The Black in Hispanic-Caribbean and Brazilian Poetry: A Comparative Perspective." *Revista/Review Interamericana* 5 (1975): 47-66.

——. "Las cualidades afrocubanas en la poesía de Nicolás Guillén." *La Torre* 18 (July-September 1970): 127-38.

Mesa-Lago, Carmelo. "Ideological, Political, and Economic Factors in the Cuban Controversy on Material Versus Moral Incentives." *Journal of Interamerican Studies and World Affairs* 14 (February 1972): 49-111.

——. "The Revolutionary Offensive." *Trans-action* 6 (April 1969): 22-29, 62.

Michalski, André. "La *Balada del Güije* de Nicolás Guillén: Un poema garcilorquiano y magicorrealista." *Cuadernos Hispanoamericanos* 274 (April 1973): 159-67.

Miller, Joseph C. "The Slave Trade in Congo and Angola." In *The African Diaspora: Interpretive Essays*, edited by Martin L. Kilson and Robert I. Rotberg. Cambridge, Mass.: Harvard University Press, 1976.

More, Carlos. "Le peuple noir a-t-il sa place dans la révolution cubaine?" *Présence Africaine* 52 (1964): 177-230.

Moreno Fraginals, Manuel. "El problema negro en la poesía cubana." *Cuadernos Hispanoamericanos* 3 (May-June 1948): 519-30.

Mullen, E. J. "Nicolás Guillén and Carlos Pellicer: A Case of Literary Parallels." *Latin American Literary Review* 3 (Spring-Summer 1975): 77-87.

Navarro Luna, Manuel. "Un líder de la poesía revolucionaria." In *Recopilación de textos sobre Nicolás Guillén*, edited by Nancy Morejón. Havana: Casa de las Américas, 1974.

Navas-Ruiz, Ricardo. "Neruda y Guillén: Un caso de relaciones literarias." *Revista Iberoamericana* 31 (July-December 1965): 251-62.

Noble, Enrique. "Aspectos étnicos y sociales de la poesía mulata hispanoamericana." *Revista Bimestre Cubana* 74 (1958): 166-79.

Pattee, Richard. "La América Latina presta atención al negro." *Revista Bimestre Cubana* 38 (1936): 17-23.

Patterson, Orlando. "Rethinking Black History." *Africa Report* 17 (November-December 1972): 29-31.

Peña, Pedro J. de la. "Tres calas en la poesía negra." *Atlántida: Revista del Pensamiento Actual* 9 (November 1971-December 1972): 798-809.

Peralta, Jaime. "España en tres poetas hispanoamericanos: Neruda, Guillén y Vallejo." *Atenea* 421-422 (July-December 1968): 37-50.

Pereda Valdés, Ildefonso. "El negro en la literatura iberoamericana." *Cuadernos* 19 (July-August 1956): 104-10.

Pereira, J. R. "Towards a Theory of Literature in Revolutionary Cuba." *Jamaica Journal* 9 (March 1975): 28-33.

Pérez-Medina, M. A. "The Situation of the Negro in Cuba." In *Negro Anthology, 1931-33*, edited by Nancy Cunard. New York: Negro Universities Press, 1969.

Polit, Carlos E. "Imagen inocente del negro en cuatro poetas antillanos." *Sin Nombre* 5 (October-December 1974): 43-60.

Portal, Magda. "Nicolás Guillén, poeta de Cuba." *Cuadernos Americanos* 197 (November-December 1974): 234-44.

Portuondo, José Antonio. "Canta a la revolución con toda la voz que tiene." In *Recopilación de textos sobre Nicolás Guillen*, edited by Nancy Morejón. Havana: Casa de las Américas, 1974.

Posada, Rafael. "La jitanjáfora revisitada." *Anales de Literatura Hispanoamericana* (Madrid) 2-3 (1973-74): 55-82.

Rabanales, Ambrosio. "Relaciones asociativas en torno al *Canto negro* de Nicolás Guillén," in *Studia Hispanica in Honorem R. Lapesa.* vol. II, pp. 469-91. Madrid: Editorial Gredos, 1974.

Rodney, Walter. "African Slavery and Other Forms of Social Oppression on the Upper Guinea Coast in the Context of the Atlantic Slave-Trade." *Journal of African History* 7 (1966): 431-43.

Rodríguez Rivera, Guillermo. "Animalia." *Casa de las Américas* 48 (May-June 1968): 138-40.

Ruscalleda Bercedóniz, Jorge María. "Apuntes para el estudio de la elegía en la poesía española e hispanoamericana." *Sin Nombre* 4 (January-March 1974): 48-56.

———. "Recuento poético de Nicolás Guillén: Homenaje en su septuagésimo aniversario." *Sin Nombre* 4 (October-December 1973): 33-56.

Ruffinelli, Jorge. "Nuevos aportes a la poesía de Nicolás Guillén. *Revista Iberoamericana de Literatura* (Montevideo) 1 (1966): 95-102.

Sánchez-Rojas, Arturo. "Papá Montero: Del son original al poema de Nicolás Guillén." *Caribe* (University of Hawaii) 5 (Fall 1976): 49-56.

Sanclemente, Álvaro. "La poesía de Nicolás Guillén." *Revista de las Indias* (Colombia) 28 (May 1946): 305-06.

Sardinha, Dennis. "Cuba—The Negrista Movement in the Process of National Integration." *Bim* 15 (June 1975): 110-17.

Schons, Dorothy. "Negro Poetry in the Americas." *Hispania* 25 (October 1942): 309-19.

Simor, András. "Algunas características comunes de un período poético de Attila József y de Nicolás Guillén." *Casa de las Américas* 100 (January-February 1977): 182-87.

Smallwood, Lawrence L., Jr. "African Cultural Dimensions in Cuba." *Journal of Black Studies* 6 (December 1975): 191-99.

Smith, M. G. "The African Heritage in the Caribbean." In *Caribbean Studies: A Symposium*, edited by Vera Rubin. Seattle: University of Washington Press, 1960.

Stevens, Evelyn P. "Machismo and Marianismo." *Society* 10 (September-October 1973): 57-63.

Torre, Guillermo de. "Literatura de color." *Revista Bimestre Cubana* 38 (1936): 5-11.

Valdés, Nelson P. "Revolution and Institutionalization in Cuba." *Cuban Studies/ Estudios Cubanos* 6 (January and July 1976): 1-37.

Waterman, Richard Alan. "African Influence on the Music of the Americas." In *Acculturation in the Americas*, edited by Sol Tax. New York: Cooper Square Publishers, 1967.

Williams, Eric. "Four Poets of the Greater Antilles." *Caribbean Quarterly* 2 (1952): 8-15.

———. "The Historical Background of Race Relations in the Caribbean," in *Miscelánea de estudios dedicados a Fernando Ortiz*. Vol. III, pp. 1525-80. Havana: Úcar García, 1956.

Williams, Lorna V. "The African Presence in the Poetry of Nicolás Guillén." In *Africa and the Caribbean: The Legacies of a Link*, edited by Margaret E. Crahan and Franklin W. Knight. Baltimore: The Johns Hopkins University Press, 1979.

Wynter, Sylvia. "Ethno or Socio Poetics." In *Alcheringa: Ethnopoetics*, edited by Michel Benamou and Jerome Rothenberg. Boston: Boston University Press, 1976.

INDEX

175